专题口译：通识篇

Thematic Interpreting: General Topics

黄珊　刘庆雪　主编

ZHEJIANG UNIVERSITY PRESS
浙江大学出版社

图书在版编目(CIP)数据

专题口译.通识篇/黄珊,刘庆雪主编. —杭州：
浙江大学出版社,2017.9(2022.6重印)
ISBN 978-7-308-17294-3

Ⅰ.①专… Ⅱ.①黄…②刘… Ⅲ.①英语—口译—自
学参考资料 Ⅳ.①H315.9

中国版本图书馆 CIP 数据核字(2017)第 196399 号

专题口译：通识篇

黄　珊　刘庆雪　主编

责任编辑	曾　熙
责任校对	徐　瑾
封面设计	周　灵
出版发行	浙江大学出版社
	（杭州市天目山路 148 号　邮政编码 310007）
	（网址：http://www.zjupress.com）
排　　版	杭州林智广告有限公司
印　　刷	杭州良诸印刷有限公司
开　　本	787mm×1092mm　1/16
印　　张	7.75
字　　数	200 千
版 印 次	2017 年 9 月第 1 版　2022 年 6 月第 4 次印刷
书　　号	ISBN 978-7-308-17294-3
定　　价	20.00 元

我们身处于一个中国走向世界、世界走向中国的伟大时代。沟通,是这一时代跨越国籍与肤色的"巴别之塔",是连接机构与企业的"融通之桥",是引领诸国合作与发展的"丝绸之路"。

2016 年 9 月 27 日,北京外国语大学中国外语测评中心推出国际人才英语考试(English Test for International Communication,简称 ETIC,即"国才考试")。国才考试以英语这一国际通用语为媒介,旨在发现不同领域、不同场景中的沟通之才,通过沟通之才实现思想流通,促进文化交流,推动社会发展,让合作更通畅,让世界更美好。

可以预测,"国才考试"将成为社会选才、用才的行业标准,帮助社会各界发现和选拔未来发展所需要的"国际人才"或"国家人才"。在这种背景之下,我们组织编写了《专题口译:通识篇》教材,旨在促进英语翻译专业学生和非英语专业高水平学生的口译技能培训和掌握。本教材充分考虑到日常口译的常见情景,涵盖了外事接待、饮食文化、礼仪祝辞、旅游观光、文化交流、商务谈判、表演艺术及社交媒体等八个不同的主题。在内容设计上,每个章节的内容包含词语预习、中译英和英译中的典型句型或者对话、中译英和英译中的段落翻译和篇章翻译、不同角度的技能训练以及相关主题的词汇拓展,并且对于篇章中出现的典型句子做了译文分析。

本书适用于英语翻译专业本科高年级学生、非英语专业高水平学生、MTI 翻译硕士低年级学生以及准备国才考试和翻译等级考试的考生。相比同类教材,本教材具有通识、实用和易操作的特点。通识是指主题内容涵盖基本社会生活;实用是指词汇和当前社会结合紧密;易操作是指内容设计合理,符合教学渐进的规律和课时分配。

《专题口译:通识篇》是华东交通大学教材(专著)基金资助项目之一,在编写过程得到了华东交通大学外国语学院的大力帮助和支持,在出版过程中得到了浙江大学出版社的大力支持,同时引用和参考了大量的网站资料以及书籍文献,在此一并致以衷心的感谢。

本书由华东交通大学外国语学院的黄珊副教授(编写了第3、4章和第8章的部分内容,约60千字)和刘庆雪副教授(编写了概论和第1、2章的内容,约65千字)主编,参与编写工作的还有刘星老师(编写了第5、6章,约32千字)、姜浩老师(编写了第7章,约20千字)和秦黎老师(编写了第8章,约18千字),以及华东交通大学2015级MTI研究生石瑛(负责了部分译文分析和词汇整理工作,约5千字)。华东交通大学外国语学院唐斌院长做了大量指导工作,浙江大学出版社曾熙做了大量编辑工作,在此表示感谢。

由于编者水平有限,书中难免有疏漏之处,敬请读者批评指正并提出宝贵意见。

编 者

2017 年 6 月 30 日

Contents 目录

概 论

Ⅰ. 口译的定义

口译的历史源远流长,作为一种在不同语言的人们之间传递信息的口头交流方式,口译活动在我国已有 2000 多年的历史。古时,从事口译职业的人被称之为"舌人""象胥"等,早在西周时期就有文献记载。数百年来西方各国虽然也有从事口译的人员,但大部分都是兼职人员,口译成为正式的专门职业是在 20 世纪初。第一次世界大战结束后的巴黎和会,由于要签订《巴黎和约》的缘故而产生了英语与法语之间的口译需求,因此大会招募了一批专职译员作连续传译(consecutive interpreting),从此口译的职业性得到了认可。而同声传译(simultaneous interpreting)则诞生于 1945 年,即第二次世界大战之后,战胜国在德国纽伦堡(Nuremberg)审判二战战犯时使用了同声传译,这也是第一次开始使用电子设备进行口译。受此启发,联合国也于 1946 年开始大量使用同声传译。1953 年,最早的一批同传译员在瑞士日内瓦成立了"国际会议口译工作者协会(L'Association Internationale des Interpretes de Conference,AIIC),这个协会的成立标志着口译职业化的正式开始。到了 21 世纪,随着经济全球化趋势的影响以及中国对外交流的日益增长,口译的重要性日益突出,口译工作者作为跨文化交际的桥梁,发挥着不可或缺的沟通作用。

口译(interpreting)是指译员(interpreter)用口头表达的方式将源语(source language)信息转换为目标语(target language)信息的即席翻译活动。

口译和笔译都是一种用不同的语言来解释和再现原文所表达思想内容的活动,虽然它们都是语言间的翻译活动,但两者之间有着显著的差异。笔译翻译的内容是确定的,译员有足够的时间可以推敲,可以查阅工具书、浏览互联网或查阅其他相关参考资料,还可以通过第三方核实、求助等方式反复斟酌修改译本。而口译则是一种具有不可预测性的即席翻译活动,需要进行现场即席翻译,译员面临较大的现场压力,译责重大。"译言既出,驷马难追",有些口译场合,如商务谈判等,口译的内容很可能千变万化,这就要求译员具有高超的即席应变能力和流利的现场表达能力。

口译的质量标准跟笔译也有区别,笔译强调"信、达、雅",口译则强调"准、顺、快"。

"准"是指完整准确地译出原话内容,所译的语言风格尽量贴近原文,无错译、漏译。错译指的是主要意思翻译错误、数字翻译严重错误、严重语体措辞错误、随意加减、严重语法错误等。漏译指主要内容或者重要细节没有给予翻译。"顺"指的是自然而流利,译语的表达要地道,符合译语的表达习惯,不拘泥于原话的词语和结构,同时表达的方式必须流畅,干脆利落而不是结结巴巴。"快"是指译员必须在说话人发言结束后的两三秒后脱口而出,及时进行口译,否则会影响口译效果,导致听众的不信任感。

口译员的单位时间劳动强度大大超过了笔译。一个小时的同声传译所处理的词语量大约是9000字,而联合国的签约笔译员每天规定的笔译工作量一般是6到8页,即2000~3000字,假定同声传译员一天工作两小时的话,词语处理量可以达到差不多20000字。这样看来,口译一天所处理的词语量大概相当于笔译的10倍。

另外书面语比较严谨,口头语比较自然、随意、松散,笔译对翻译思维的周密性、用词的准确性、结构的严谨性,要求比较高,而口译则对译员思维敏捷性、随机应变能力要求比较高。例如,在翻译"他吃得很多。"时,笔译可以翻译为"He has a good appetite.",而口译则只要翻译为"He eats a lot."即可。

Ⅱ. 口译的分类

口译从操作方式上主要可以分为同声传译(simultaneous interpreting)和交替传译(consecutive interpreting)。同声传译是指译员在不打断讲话者发言的情况下,几乎同步地将其讲话内容传译给听众。译员需要边听边译,边译边听,口头译着一句话,耳朵同时听着下一句,大脑同时快速地分析、转换,发言者发言一结束,传译也几乎同时完成。交替翻译是指一种讲话人说完一句话、几句话或一段话,停下来让译员进行传译的口译方式,讲话与翻译交替进行。讲话的时间可以从几秒到几分钟不等,译员在讲话者的自然停顿间隙,将信息一组一组地传译给听众。另外口译还有耳语口译(whispering interpreting)和视译(sight interpreting)。耳语口译,是指译员用耳语的方式轻轻把信息传译给另一方,耳语口译的听众一般是少数人,适用于大多数人懂一种语言,而少数听众(最多两到三个)不懂这种语言的情况,故需要译员为其单独进行口译,也称为"咬耳朵"翻译。视译则是指用阅读的方式来接收源语信息,即一面看原文讲稿,一面口译出材料的内容。

口译按其服务的场合,可分成会议口译、陪同口译、法庭口译、医疗口译等。会议口译(conference interpreting),是指为会议配备的口译,主要采取同声传译或连续传译的方式。陪同口译(escort interpreting),是指译员陪同外宾或者代表团进行旅游、购物、参观等活动。法庭口译(court interpreting),是指为司法场合配备的口译,一般是指在民事或刑事诉讼过程中,当事人或证人由于不通晓当地(国)的通用/官方语言造成理解和表达上的困难时所得到的翻译服务。医疗口译(medical interpreting)，是指为有需要的人员提供医疗服务时配备的口译，对译员在医疗服务专业方面的知识有一定的要求，所以也被单列为一种口译类型。

Ⅲ. 译员的素质要求

译员首先要具备扎实的语言(双语)基础，熟练掌握各种口译技巧，具有敏锐的口译听辨能力，较强的脑记和笔记能力，流利的双语表达能力。其次，译员还需要具有丰富的语言外知识，包括百科知识和专业主题知识。由于需要口译的内容包罗万象，上到天文下到地理，古今中外都有可能涉及，译员需要有广博的知识面。译员还需要有灵敏的现场反应能力。因为现场情况千变万化，即使译员准备得非常充分，都有可能遇上困境，这就要求译员能灵活应变，具备一定的现场应变能力。口译是发生在不同文化背景之间的交际活动，文化冲突是必然的，所以译员还需要具有跨文化交际的意识，以克服由于文化背景不同而产生的交流障碍。

一名合格的译员还需要有过硬的身体素质和心理素质，能承受强大的工作压力，具备严格的职业素养，能对所翻译的资料和会议内容严格保密，具有良好的口译服务职业道德和合作精神。

第一章 外事接待

Ⅰ. 词汇预习

jet lag 时差

give a banquet in somebody's honor 设宴洗尘

tentative itinerary 初步拟定的活动日程

Silk Road Economic Belt and 21st-Century Maritime Silk Road ("Belt and Road") "丝绸之路经济带"和"21世纪海上丝绸之路"("一带一路")

Yang Pass 阳关

Gobi Desert 戈壁

West Region 西域

rejuvenation 复兴

dovetail 吻合

converge 聚合

initiative 首创

the concerted efforts 共同努力

unprecedented 前所未有的

be privileged to 很荣幸

captivate 迷住

pressing 急迫的

steward 组织者

Ⅱ. 典型句型

1. 中译英

（1）很高兴出席由中国旅游协会和《中国旅游》杂志社联合举办的国际旅游合作论坛。

It gives me great pleasure to attend the international tourism cooperation forum， co-organized by China Tourism Association and *China Tourism* magazine.

（2）有朋自远方来，不亦乐乎。干杯！为我们的友谊干杯！

It's wonderful to have friends visiting us from afar. Cheers! To our friendship!

（3）借此机会，我代表我们代表团的全体成员，对东道主的诚挚邀请，表示真诚的谢意。

On behalf of all the members of my mission，I would like to take this opportunity to express our sincere thanks to our host for their earnest invitation.

（4）谢谢您亲自专程赶来接待我。

Thank you very much for coming all the way to meet me in person.

（5）久仰，久仰！

I have long been looking forward to meeting you.

2. 英译中

（1）Do you have much trouble with the jet lag?

你会不会还不太适应时差？

（2）Ladies and gentlemen，I would like to take great pleasure in introducing our distinguished guest，Dr. White.

女士们、先生们，我非常荣幸地向各位介绍我们的贵宾怀特博士。

（3）Thank you all for this warm welcome. It is always a pleasure for me to come to Nanchang and to see at first-hand its ongoing transformation.

感谢大家的热烈欢迎。很高兴有机会到南昌，亲眼看到南昌正在发生的变化。

（4）I wish you a pleasant journey and don't forget to keep in touch.

祝你旅途愉快，别忘了保持联系。

（5）We are sorry that we shall be leaving very soon. It's really a most interesting and rewarding visit.

非常遗憾我们马上要离开（贵公司）了。说真的，这次访问非常有意思，非常有收获。

Ⅲ. 对话翻译

A：Excuse me! Are you Mr. Smith from Chicago International Trading Corporation?

（请问，您是芝加哥国际贸易公司的史密斯先生吗？）

B：Yes. I am.

（是的，我是。）

A：见到您很高兴，史密斯先生，我叫李梅，我是南昌新华贸易公司的销售部经理，我来这接您。

（Nice to meet you，Mr. Smith. My name is Li Mei. I'm the sales manager of

Nanchang Xinhua Trading Company. I'm here to meet you.)

B：How do you do，Ms. Li?

（您好，李女士。）

A：您好，史密斯先生，欢迎您来南昌！

（How do you do，Mr. Smith? Welcome to Nanchang!）

B：Thank you. It's very kind of you to come to meet me at the airport，Ms. Li.

（谢谢李女士！谢谢您到机场来接我。）

A：不客气。希望您此次访问愉快。

（It's my pleasure. I hope you will have a nice stay here.）

B：Thank you. I am sure I will.

（谢谢，一定会的。）

A：我们的车在外边等我们，您要先去取下行李吗？

（Our car is just expecting us outside there. Do you need to get back your luggage?）

B：Yes.

（好的。）

A：车开过来了，我们边走边聊吧。这是您第一次来南昌吗？

（Here comes the car. Shall we go and talk on the way to the hotel? Is this your first visit to Nanchang?）

B：Yes. Actually，it's my first time here.

（是的，这是我第一次到南昌。）

A：我们到了，您可以在宾馆休息一下，我六点钟来接您，我们设宴为您洗尘，然后会介绍一下初步拟定的活动日程。

（Here we are. You can have a rest in the hotel and I will pick you up at six o'clock for the reception banquet in your honor and will give you an account of tentative itinerary then.）

B：OK，thank you for your thoughtful arrangement. See you later.

（好的，谢谢你们的周到安排，再见。）

Ⅳ. 篇章翻译

1. 中译英

【原文】

很高兴和大家相聚在兰州这座美丽的黄河之都。①首先，我代表中国外交部对亚洲合作对话（ACD）丝绸之路务实合作论坛的举行表示热烈祝贺，对参加本次论坛的国内外嘉宾表示诚挚的欢迎,也请大家与我一道,以掌声对甘肃省为论坛所做的周到安排表示衷心感谢。

本次论坛的主题是亚洲合作和丝绸之路。2000多年前,中国的先人不畏艰辛,跋山涉水,在欧亚大陆及其沿海开辟了陆海两条丝绸之路。甘肃省位于陆上丝绸之路的黄金段,中国的先人曾从这里出阳关、越戈壁、赴西域,与沿线各国人民互通有无,和睦共处,留下许多脍炙人口的传说和佳话。

②丝绸之路是和平之路、友谊之路、合作之路,是沿线国家友好交往的历史见证,是亚洲国家共同的珍贵遗产和宝贵财富。当前,亚洲已成为世界发展的重要引擎,古老的大陆正迎来新的伟大复兴。中国领导人倡议亚洲国家共建"丝绸之路经济带"和"21世纪海上丝绸之路",其要义就是弘扬丝绸之路精神,拓展亚洲区域合作,让亚洲的发展为世界的繁荣作出更大的贡献。

今天,亚洲合作对话成员代表,齐聚兰州,重拾丝绸之路精神,共促亚洲合作进程。这既是对历史的传承,也是对未来的期许,意义深远,使命崇高。

"一带一路"是中国的倡议,更是亚洲国家共同的事业。亚洲合作对话是我们推进泛亚合作的重要机制,更是我们共建"一带一路"的重要平台。我坚信,在各方共同努力下,亚洲合作对话将为"一带一路"建设增添动力,同样,"一带一路"建设也将进一步丰富亚洲合作对话的内涵,并为亚洲腾飞插上强劲的翅膀。

最后,我预祝明天的论坛圆满成功!

谢谢大家!

【译文】

It's such a delight to be with you in Lanzhou, a beautiful city on the Yellow River. ①On behalf of the Ministry of Foreign Affairs of China, let me, first of all, extend warm congratulations on the opening of the ACD Forum on Silk Road Cooperation and a hearty welcome to the Chinese and foreign guests. May I now invite you to express, with a round of applause, our sincere thanks to Gansu Province for the thoughtful arrangements.

The theme of the Forum is Asian cooperation and the Silk Road. Over two thousand years ago, the ancestors of the Chinese people traveled across mountains and rivers in defiance of difficulties and hardships to open the Silk Road, with one route spanning the Eurasian continent and the other along its coast. Gansu Province sits on the prime passage of the land route of the Silk Road. This is where our forefathers crossed the Yang Pass and started their journeys to the West Region. Along the route across the Gobi Desert, they traded and interacted with locals, leaving behind a trail of widely told stories of mutual respect, amity and harmony.

②The Silk Road，a road of peace，friendship，and cooperation，has borne witness to the friendly exchanges among the countries along the routes. It is an invaluable legacy and asset shared by all Asian countries. Asia，an ancient continent and major engine of world growth，is on its way to new，great rejuvenation. The Chinese leader has proposed building with other Asian countries the Silk Road Economic Belt and the 21st-Century Maritime Silk Road（known as the "Belt and Road"）to promote the Silk Road spirit and expand regional cooperation in Asia，so that Asia will contribute more to world prosperity through its own development.

Today，delegates of ACD members are gathered in Lanzhou to revive the Silk Road spirit and promote Asian cooperation. This is a lofty mission，a mission that builds on history and looks to the future，and will produce far-reaching impact.

The "Belt and Road" is China's initiative and，more importantly，a common cause of all Asian countries. The ACD is both a major mechanism for pushing forward pan-Asia cooperation and a significant platform for building the "Belt and Road". I am confident that with the concerted efforts of all parties，the ACD will give a strong boost to the building of the "Belt and Road". Likewise，the "Belt and Road"，as they progress，will also enrich the ACD and lend wings to Asia's powerful takeoff in the world.

To conclude，may I wish tomorrow's Forum a great success.

Thank you.

【译文分析】

①首先,我代表中国外交部对亚洲合作对话(ACD)丝绸之路务实合作论坛的举行表示热烈祝贺,对参加本次论坛的国内外嘉宾表示诚挚的欢迎,也请大家与我一道,以掌声对甘肃省为论坛所做的周到安排表示衷心感谢。

译文：On behalf of the Ministry of Foreign Affairs of China，let me，first of all，extend warm congratulations on the opening of the ACD Forum on Silk Road Cooperation and a hearty welcome to the Chinese and foreign guests. May I now invite you to express，with a round of applause，our sincere thanks to Gansu Province for the thoughtful arrangements.

中文的长句可以进行断句,合并,在这个句子中,"对……表示热烈祝贺,对……表示诚挚的欢迎"合并为一个句子,"extend warm congratulations on... and a hearty welcome to...",而后面的"对……周到安排表示衷心感谢"处理成另外一个句子"May I now invite you to express，with a round of applause，our sincere thanks to...".

②丝绸之路是和平之路、友谊之路、合作之路,是沿线国家友好交往的历史见证,是

亚洲国家共同的珍贵遗产和宝贵财富。

译文：The Silk Road，a road of peace，friendship，and cooperation，has borne witness to the friendly exchanges among the countries along the routes. It is an invaluable legacy and asset shared by all Asian countries.

中文句型中常有重复之处，翻译成英语时可以省略，如此句中的"和平之路、友谊之路、合作之路"译为"a road of peace，friendship，and cooperation"，"珍贵遗产和宝贵财富"则译为"an invaluable legacy and asset"。

2. 英译中

【原文】

Mr. President，Prince Philip and I are delighted to welcome you and Madame Peng to Buckingham Palace this evening.

Your visit to the United Kingdom marks a milestone in this unprecedented year of cooperation and friendship between the United Kingdom and China，as we celebrate the ties between our two countries and prepare to take them to ambitious new heights.

The United Kingdom and China have a warm and longstanding friendship. Prince Philip and I recall with great fondness our visit to China almost thirty years ago，where we were privileged to experience your country's rich history and culture，including the Great Wall，the Forbidden City and the Terracotta Warriors：all unforgettable memories of China's ancient civilization.

①Yet it was China's desire to shape a new future which captivated us most. We were struck by the energy and enthusiasm with which China's leaders were forging ahead with a new and ambitious future for the Chinese people；and ②I well recall our discussions with the late paramount leader Mr. Deng Xiaoping，who was foremost among these leaders in setting a clear direction for China with his policy of reform. It was also Mr. Deng's visionary concept of One Country Two Systems that opened the way for China's restoration of sovereignty over Hong Kong under the Sino-British Joint Declaration.

Almost thirty years later，Mr. Deng's vision has borne remarkable fruit. Rapid economic growth and development has transformed the lives of people across China and lifted hundreds of millions out of poverty：a huge and historic achievement with far-reaching positive effects on people's lives.

I was delighted that my grandson Prince William was able to witness these changes during his first visit to China earlier this year. Like myself and Prince Philip，he visited not only your great cities of Beijing and Shanghai but also the beautiful province of Yunnan，and saw at first-hand the strong connections which bind our two countries together，be they in culture，education or business.

Mr. President，the relationship between the United Kingdom and China is now truly a global partnership. We have much reason to celebrate the dynamic，growing economic relationship between our countries as well as our success in working together to address pressing international challenges.

We have，this year，marked the seventieth anniversary of the foundation of the United Nations. Today the world faces challenges which call for collaboration between the nations：conflict and terrorism；poverty and ill-health；conservation and climate change. As permanent members of the United Nations Security Council，Britain and China are stewards of the rules-based international system，and we have a responsibility to cooperate on these issues which have a direct bearing on the security and prosperity of all our peoples.

This global partnership is supported by an expanding network of links between the people of our two countries，which are essential in building mutual understanding and friendship，while we welcome the increasing numbers of Chinese tourists，students and business visitors to the United Kingdom.

Mr. President，your visit is a defining moment in this very special year for our bilateral relationship. I am confident that it will serve to highlight the sincerity and warmth of our friendship and to strengthen relations between our countries for many years to come.

Ladies and Gentlemen，I ask you to rise and drink a toast to the President and Madame Peng and to the people of China.

【译文】

主席先生,菲利普亲王和我本人非常高兴地欢迎您和您的夫人彭丽媛女士今晚来白金汉宫做客。

您对英国的访问是一个重要的里程碑,标志着今年英中两国合作和友谊达到了前所未有的高度。我们要庆祝两国之间的友好关系,并将其推向雄心勃勃的新高度。

英中两国一直保持着长久友好的关系。我和菲利普亲王经常会重温将近30年前我们那次访问中国的美好回忆。我们很荣幸能够体验贵国的丰富历史和文化,如长城、故宫和兵马俑等,中国的这些古代文明都给我们留下了难忘的回忆。

①而让我们印象最为深刻的是中国塑造崭新未来的愿望。中国领导人为带领中国人民走向一个雄心勃勃的新未来所展现的能量和热情,让我们感受颇深。②我清楚地记得我与已故重要领导人邓小平先生的会晤,邓先生高瞻远瞩地为中国的改革政策指明了

方向。也正是邓小平先生"一国两制"的远见卓识，为在《中英联合声明》下的中国对香港恢复行使主权开辟了道路。

将近30年后，邓先生的愿景已取得了丰硕的成果。中国快速的经济增长和发展，改变了全体中国人民的生活，使数亿人民摆脱了贫困。这是一个巨大的历史性成就，对人们的生活产生了深远的积极影响。

我感到高兴的是，今年早些时候，我的孙儿——威廉王子——在他第一次访问中国期间能够目睹这些变化。与我和菲利普亲王一样，他不仅访问了中国的伟大城市北京和上海，而且还去了美丽的云南，亲身体验了促进我们两国关系紧密发展的诸多领域，无论是文化、教育，还是商业领域。

主席先生，英国和中国之间的关系现在是一种真正的全球伙伴关系。我们有充分的理由来庆祝两国之间活跃的、不断增长的经济关系，以及我们在共同应对紧迫的国际性挑战方面所取得的成功。

今年是联合国成立70周年。今天世界所面临的挑战需要各国之间的协作来加以应对：冲突和恐怖主义、贫困和健康不良、资源保护和气候变化。作为联合国安全理事会的常任理事国，英国和中国都是以规则为基础的国际体系的维护者，我们有责任就这些直接关系到两国人民的安全和繁荣的问题携手合作。

这一全球伙伴关系是建立在两国人民之间不断扩大的联系网络基础上的，这种联系对于构建相互理解和友谊至关重要。我们欢迎越来越多的中国游客、学生和商务访客前来英国。

主席先生，今年对于英中两国双边关系来说是非常特殊的一年，您的访问是一个决定性的时刻。我相信，这将有助于突显两国之间的真诚和温馨的友谊，加强未来两国之间的长久友好关系。

女士们，先生们，我请大家起立，共同举杯，为习近平主席和夫人彭丽媛女士的健康、为中国人民的健康与幸福，干杯。

【译文分析】

①Yet it was China's desire to shape a new future which captivated us most.

译文：而让我们印象最为深刻的是中国塑造崭新未来的愿望。

英汉属于不同语系，定语的位置虽有相同之处但也有差异，英语中定语从句后置，译成中文需要调整语序，必要时也需调整句子成分，如在此句中则把定语从句"which captivated us most"转换为主语从句"让我们印象最为深刻"，并置为句首。

②I well recall our discussions with the late paramount leader Mr. Deng Xiaoping, who was foremost among these leaders in setting a clear direction for China with his policy of reform.

译文：我清楚地记得我与已故重要领导人邓小平先生的会晤，邓先生高瞻远瞩地为中国的改革政策指明了方向。

英语中的定语从句均为后置定语,如果从句太长,翻译成中文时可以进行断句,分成两个句子,再把"who"所指代的成分"邓小平先生"重复一遍。

Ⅴ. 技能训练之听辨理解

著名的口译专家 Gile 在认知概念的基础上提出了同声传译和交替传译的脑力分配模式。他指出同声传译的脑力分配模式为:SI＝L＋M＋P＋C,即同声传译(simultaneous interpreting)＝听力与分析(listening and analysis)＋短期记忆(short term memory)＋言语表达(speech production)＋协调(coordination)。而交替传译的脑力分配模式分成两个阶段:Phase I 为 CI＝L＋N＋M＋C,Phase II 为 CI＝Rem＋Read＋P,即连续传译(consecutive interpreting)(第一阶段)＝听力与分析(listening and analysis)＋笔记(note taking)＋短期记忆(short term memory)＋协调(coordination),连续传译(第二阶段)＝记忆(remembering)＋读笔记(note reading)＋传达(production)。从这里可以看出,无论是同声传译还是交替传译,听辨理解能力都是进行口译活动的第一步。

口译听辨的目的是充分理解源语发言人的意思,这就要求译员不能单纯地听词,而必须听意,在听辨的过程中,我们要不断地问自己"发言人想要表达什么意思",运用语言知识进行语法和语用的分析的同时,充分激活与主题相关的言外知识进行分析。

在连续传译中,我们需要去识别主题信息,主题信息一般由主题句和句中的关键词构成,英语语篇的主题句往往出现在语段的开头,而句中的关键词一般体现为句中的实词,尤其是充当主语、谓语、宾语的实词,因此在听辨的过程中我们要以意群为单位进行听辨,以语块(chunks)化方式摄取信息,扩展听幅(span of listening comprehension),注意提取意群中的关键词,把握句子的意思。在词汇层面,注意名词、动词、形容词等实词;在句法层面注意主语、谓语、宾语或表语等句子的主干结构;在语篇方面要注意抓住逻辑线索;在语意层面注意把握已知信息和新信息;在语气层面注意说话人的重读、强调和重复。请读以下段落,用单斜线"/"对句子进行意群切分。

Relations between the United States and France appeared to grow stronger this week after President Francois Hollande visited Washington. President Barack Obama welcomed the French leader by taking him on Monday to Charlottesville, Virginia. They visited Monticello, the 18th century house designed and built by Thomas Jefferson, America's third president. Jefferson was also one of the writers of the Declaration of Independence and served as America's representative to France from 1785 to 1789. President Obama told President Hollande that Monticello is an example of what he called the "incredible history" between the United States and France. Thomas Jefferson loved France，and was a supporter of the French Revolution. As Mr. Obama noted，France supported Britain's North American colonies as they fought for independence.

【参考】

Relations between the United States and France/appeared to grow stronger/this week/after President Francois Hollande/visited/Washington.//President Barack Obama welcomed the French leader/by taking him on Monday to Charlottesville，Virginia.//They visited Monticello，/the 18th century house designed and built by Thomas Jefferson，/America's third president.//Jefferson was also one of the writers of the Declaration of Independence/and served as America's representative to France from 1785 to 1789.//President Obama told President Hollande/that Monticello is an example/of what he called the "incredible history"/between the United States and France.//Thomas Jefferson loved France，/and was a supporter of the French Revolution.//As Mr. Obama noted，/France supported Britain's North American colonies/as they fought for independence.//

Ⅵ. 词汇拓展

接机服务 meeting service

国际出发/抵达 international departure/arrival

机场大楼 terminal building

候机大厅 waiting hall

问讯处 information desk/inquiry desk

起飞时间 departure time/takeoff time

抵达时间 arrival time

登机卡 boarding ticket/boarding pass

安全检查 security check

海关 the Customs

办理海关例行手续 go through customs formalities

报关 make a customs declaration

海关行李申报表 baggage declaration form/luggage declaration form

往返票 round-trip ticket/return ticket

入/出/过境签证 entry/exit/transit visa

一次性入境/多次入境/再入境签证 single entry/multiple-entry/re-entry visa

旅游签证 tourist visa

免签证明 visa waiver

外交护照 diplomatic passport

公务护照 service passport

免税商店 duty-free shop

转机 interline connection；trans-boarding

中转处 transfer correspondence

行李提取处 baggage claim/luggage claim

手提行李 hand luggage

随身携带行李 carry-on baggage

行李标签牌 baggage tag/luggage tag

行李寄存处 baggage depositary/luggage depositary

行李手推车 baggage handcart/luggage pushcart

机场行李搬运工 skycap

机场班车 airport shuttle bus

健康证书 health certificate

种疫苗证书 vaccination certificate

预防接种证书 inoculation certificate

盛大招待会 grand reception

旅馆登记表 hotel registration form

旅馆休息大厅 hotel lobby/hotel lounge

旅馆服务员 attendant

总统套房 presidential suite

豪华套房 luxury suite

单人房间 single room

双人房间 double room

举行盛大招待会 hold a grand reception

答谢招待会 reciprocal reception

冷餐招待会 buffet reception

感谢热情招待 thank you for your kind hospitality

招待所 guest house

紧凑的活动安排 tight schedule/busy schedule

精心的安排 thoughtful arrangements

详细介绍活动安排 give a detailed account of the schedule

欢迎辞 welcome speech/welcome address

告别辞 farewell speech/farewell address

合作共事 work as your colleague

亲眼目睹 witness with my own eyes

专程赶来 come all the way

若有不便 encounter any inconveniences

参与我们的项目 participate in our project

促进友谊 promote friendship

加强合作 enhance cooperation

不辞辛劳远道来访 come in spite of the long and tiring journey

短暂的访问 brief visit

有此殊荣 have the honor of doing something

很高兴做某事 have the pleasure in doing something

请允许我介绍 may I present somebody/allow me to introduce...

请你不要介意 hope you don't mind

祝你参观顺利 wish you a pleasant visit

祝你访问圆满成功 wish your visit a complete success

祝你万事如意 wish you all the best

送别 see somebody off

期待再次来访 look forward to your visit again

希望再次相会 hope to see each other again soon

代我向某某问好 say hello to... for me

请多保重 take care

视你旅途愉快 wish you a pleasant journey/have a nice trip

一路平安 bon voyage/have a safe trip home

参考文献

［1］http：//www.fmprc.gov.cn/web/.

［2］http：//www.hxen.com/englishlistening/voaenglish/voaspecialenglish/2014-02-15/329101_4.html.

第二章 饮食文化

Ⅰ. 词汇预习

rice dumplings wrapped in reed leaves 粽子

cuisine 烹饪,烹调法

imperial 皇帝的,帝国的

aroma 香味

shrimp cocktail 鲜虾盅,鸡尾冷虾

napkin 餐巾

steamed pork with rice flour 粉蒸肉

stewed chicken with three cups of sauce 三杯鸡

braised pork with dried bamboo shoots 笋干烧肉

crock soup 瓦罐汤

mouthwatering 令人垂涎的;美味的

greasy 油腻的

crisp 脆的,酥的

shallot 大葱

garlic 大蒜

pungent 辛辣的

thin soup 清汤

creamy soup 油汤

deep-fry 炸

grill 烤

stir-fry 炒

prickly ash 花椒

fermented soybean 豆豉

hot pot 火锅

raptor 猛禽

sauté 煸炒

meticulous 精细的

bland（食物）淡而无味的

crescent 新月;新月形的

vacuum-packed 真空包装的

congee 粥,稀饭

soy milk 豆浆

barrel 桶

Ⅱ. 典型句型

1. 中译英

（1）中国的哲学家老子曾经说过:"治大国如烹小鲜。"

The great Chinese philosopher Lao-tzu once said，"Governing a great nation is much like cooking a small fish."

（2）我想来点清淡些的,你能推荐什么吗?

I prefer something light. What would you recommend?

（3）——我们各付各的吧。

——不,这次我请客。

—Let me pay my share.

—No，it's my treat.

（4）端午节吃粽子、赛龙舟是我们的习俗。

It has been our tradition to eat rice dumplings wrapped in reed leaves and hold dragon boat races during the Dragon Boat Festival season.

（5）作为我国北方菜系的代表,鲁菜烹饪技术广泛用于明清两代的宫廷菜。

Shandong cuisine is the representative of northern China's cooking and its technique has been widely absorbed by the imperial dishes of the Ming（1368—1644）and Qing（1616—1911）dynasties.

2. 英译中

（1）The three criteria generally used to judge Chinese cooking are color，aroma and taste.

中国饮食的评判标准讲究色、香、味。

（2）Keep your mouth closed while chewing，and makes as little noise as possible.

咀嚼食物时要双唇紧闭,尽量不要发出声音。

（3）Would you like to have a la carte or buffet?

你喜欢照菜单点菜还是吃自助餐?

（4）I'd like to start with shrimp cocktail，then the steak. I'll have a sundae for dessert，and some black coffee.

先给我上个鸡尾冷虾,然后上牛排,再来个圣代当甜点,还要清咖啡。

（5）You'd better not leave the napkin on the table. Put it on your lap where it's supposed to protect your clothes from spilled food or used to wipe your hands or mouth when necessary.

最好不把餐巾放在餐桌上,而是把它放在膝盖上,用来保护你的衣服不被食物溅脏,或者需要时用来擦手或嘴。

Ⅲ. 对话翻译

At a dinner party
在宴会上

A：Mr. White，take a seat，please.

（怀特先生,请坐。）

B：Thank you.

（谢谢。）

A：What would you like to drink，beer，wine or Site?

（你想喝点什么,啤酒,葡萄酒,还是四特?）

B：What is Site?

（四特是什么?）

A：It's a kind of spirits，a Jiangxi specialty，but it is a bit strong.

（它是一种烈性酒,江西特产,但是度数有点偏高。）

B：In that case，I'd prefer beer.

（那么,我喝啤酒。）

A：But it is said that it will be a pity if you leave Jiangxi without drinking Site.

（但是一些人说,如果不喝四特酒而离开江西,是一件非常遗憾的事。）

B：Really? OK，I'll take a sip later.

（真的吗? 好吧,我等会尝一点。）

A：What would you like，Chinese food or Western food?

（你是想吃中餐,还是西餐?）

B：Chinese food，please.

（中餐吧。）

A：Would you like to use chopsticks?

（你想用筷子吗？）

B：Yes，of course. As the saying goes，when in Rome，do as the Romans do. Although I can't get along with them，I'd like to learn to handle them.

（当然想，俗话说入乡随俗。尽管我不会用筷子，但我想学着用它们。）

A：因为这是你第一次来到江西，我想给你介绍一些典型的江西特色菜。

（Since this is the first time for you to come to Jiangxi，I'd like to recommend some traditional Jiangxi dishes to you.）

C：你们现在可以点菜了吗？

（Are you ready for your order?）

B：Yes，steamed pork with rice flour，stewed chicken with three cups of sauce，braised pork with dried bamboo shoots，crock soup，and two tins of Nanchang beer.

（粉蒸肉、三杯鸡、笋干烧肉、瓦罐汤，以及两听南昌啤酒。）

C：我马上就把菜端来。

（I'll get the dishes for you right now.）

After the dishes are served

上菜后

A：Please help yourselves to what you like. Let's drink the beer. Here is to your health.

（请随便吃菜。我们喝啤酒吧。为你的健康干杯！）

B：And to our friendship and cooperation. The dishes are really delicious.

（为我们的友谊和合作干杯！这些菜真是诱人。）

A：I'm glad that you like the Chinese food. Have some more soup，please.

（我很高兴你喜欢中国菜。多喝点汤吧。）

B：I'm afraid I've had enough.

（我觉得我已经饱了。）

A：Some more dishes?

（还要点什么吗？）

B：No，thanks. I'm full. Thank you for the wonderful dinner.

（不，谢谢，我吃饱了。谢谢你这顿精美的晚餐。）

A：Don't mention it.

（不客气。）

Ⅳ. 篇章翻译

1. 中译英

【原文】

①中国地域辽阔,民族众多,因此各种中国饮食口味不同,却都味美,令人垂涎。因为中国地方菜肴各具特色,总体来讲,中国饮食可以大致分为八大地方菜系:山东菜系、四川菜系、广东菜系、福建菜系、江苏菜系、浙江菜系、湖南菜系和安徽菜系。

山东菜系

许多山东菜的历史和孔夫子一样悠久,使得山东菜系成为中国现存的最古老的主要菜系之一。②山东菜系由济南菜系和胶东菜系组成,清淡,不油腻,以其香、鲜、酥、软而闻名。因为使用青葱和大蒜做为调料,山东菜系通常很辣。

四川菜系

四川菜系,是世界上最著名的中国菜系之一。四川菜系以其香辣而闻名,味道多变,着重使用红辣椒,搭配使用青椒和花椒,产生出经典的刺激的味道。此外,大蒜、姜和豆豉也被应用于烹饪。油炸、无油炸、腌制和文火炖煮是基本的烹饪技术。四川火锅也许是世界上最出名的火锅,尤其是半辣半清的鸳鸯火锅。

广东菜系

广东菜源自于中国最南部的省份广东省。大多数华侨来自广东,因此广东菜也许是国外最广泛的中国地方菜系。广东菜是品种丰富的中国菜系之一,使用很多来自世界其他地方的蔬菜,很少使用辣椒,而是注重保持蔬菜和肉类自身的风味。广东菜,味道清、淡、脆、鲜,为西方人所熟知,常用猛禽走兽来烹饪出有创意的菜肴。它的基础烹饪方法包括烤、炒、煸、深炸、烤、炖和蒸。

福建菜系

福建菜系由福州菜、泉州菜和厦门菜组成,以其精选的海鲜,漂亮的色泽,以及甜、酸、咸和香的味道而出名。最特别的是它的"卤味"。

江苏菜系

江苏菜以水产作为主要原料,注重原料的鲜味。其雕刻技术十分珍贵,其中瓜雕尤其著名。烹饪技术包括炖、烤、焙、煨等。江苏菜的特色是淡、鲜、甜、雅。江苏菜系以其精选的原料,精细的准备,不辣不温的口感而出名。因为江苏气候变化很大,江苏菜系在一年之中也有变化。

浙江菜系

浙江菜系由杭州菜、宁波菜和绍兴菜组成,不油腻,以其菜肴的鲜、柔、滑、香而闻名。杭州菜是这三者中最出名的一个。

湖南菜系

湖南菜系由湘江地区、洞庭湖和湘西的地方菜肴组成。它以其极辣的味道为特色。红辣椒、青辣椒和青葱是这一菜系中的必备品。

安徽菜系

安徽厨师注重于烹饪的温度,擅长煨炖。通常会加入火腿和方糖来改善菜肴的味道。

【译文】

①China covers a large territory and has many nationalities, hence having a variety of Chinese food with different but fantastic and mouthwatering flavor. Since China's local dishes have their own typical characteristics, generally, Chinese food can be roughly divided into eight regional cuisines, which are Shandong cuisine, Sichuan cuisine, Guangdong cuisine, Fujian cuisine, Jiangsu cuisine, Zhejiang cuisine, Hunan cuisine, and Anhui cuisine.

Shandong Cuisine

Much of Shandong cuisine's history is as old as Confucius himself, making it one of the oldest existing major cuisines in China. ② Consisting of Jinan cuisine and Jiaodong cuisine, Shandong cuisine, clear, pure and not greasy, is characterized by its emphasis on aroma, freshness, crispness and tenderness. Shallot and garlic are usually used as seasonings so Shangdong dishes tastes pungent usually. Soups are given much emphasis in Shangdong dishes.

Sichuan Cuisine

Sichuan cuisine, is one of the most famous Chinese cuisines in the world. Characterized by its spicy and pungent flavor, Sichuan cuisine, prolific of tastes, emphasizes on the use of chili. Pepper and prickly ash also never fail to accompany, producing typical exciting tastes. Besides, garlic, ginger and fermented soybean are also used in the cooking process. Frying, frying without oil, pickling and braising are applied as basic cooking techniques. Sichuan hot pots are perhaps the most famous hotpots in the world, most notably the Yuan Yang(mandarin duck) Hotpot, half spicy and half clear.

Guangdong Cuisine

Canton food originates from Guangdong, the southernmost province in China. The majority of overseas Chinese people are from Guangdong (Canton) so Cantonese is perhaps the most widely available Chinese regional cuisine outside of China. Cantonese food is one of the most diverse and richest cuisines in China. Many vegetables originate from other parts of the world. It doesn't use much spice, bringing out the natural flavor of the vegetables and meats. Tasting clear, light, crisp and fresh, Guangdong cuisine, familiar to Westerners, usually chooses raptors and beasts to produce originative dishes. Its basic cooking techniques include roasting, stir-frying, sautéing, deep-frying, braising, stewing and steaming.

Fujian Cuisine

Consisting of Fuzhou cuisine, Quanzhou cuisine and Xiamen cuisine, Fujian cuisine is distinguished for its choice seafood, beautiful color and magic taste of sweet, sour, salty and savory. The most distinct features are their "pickled taste".

Jiangsu Cuisine

Aquatics as the main ingredients, Jiangsu cuisine stresses the freshness of materials. Its carving techniques are delicate, of which the melon carving technique is especially well known. Cooking techniques consist of stewing, braising, roasting, simmering, etc. Its flavor is light, fresh and sweet and with delicate elegance. Jiangsu cuisine is well known for its careful selection of ingredients, its meticulous preparation methodology, and its not-too-spicy, not-too-bland taste. Since the seasons vary in climate considerably in Jiangsu, the cuisine also varies throughout the year.

Zhejiang Cuisine

Comprising local cuisines of Hangzhou, Ningbo and Shaoxing, Zhejiang cuisine, not greasy, wins its reputation for freshness, tenderness, softness, smoothness of its dishes with mellow fragrance. Hangzhou cuisine is the most famous one among the three.

Hunan Cuisine

Hunan cuisine consists of local Cuisines of Xiangjiang Region, Dongting Lake and Xiangxi coteau. It characterizes itself by thick and pungent flavor. Chili, pepper and shallot are usually necessaries in this division.

Anhui Cuisine

Anhui cuisine chefs focus much more attention on the temperature in cooking and are good at braising and stewing. Often hams and sugar will be added to improve taste.

【译文分析】

①中国地域辽阔,民族众多,因此各种中国饮食口味不同,却都味美,令人垂涎。

译文:China covers a large territory and has many nationalities, hence having a variety of Chinese food with different but fantastic and mouthwatering flavor.

中文中的形容词可以作谓语,翻译成英文时要注意加上 be 动词或者进行句子成分转换,如"地域辽阔,民族众多"可以翻译为"...covers a large territory and has many nationalities","口味不同,味美,令人垂涎"可以转换成定语结构"a variety of Chinese food with different but fantastic and mouthwatering flavor"。

②山东菜系由济南菜系和胶东菜系组成,清淡,不油腻,以其香、鲜、酥、软而闻名。

译文: Consisting of Jinan cuisine and Jiaodong cuisine, Shandong cuisine, clear, pure and not greasy, is characterized by its emphasis on aroma, freshness, crispness and tenderness.

中文中的几个并列简单句,可以翻译成英语中的一个复杂结构的主句。此中文句中的谓语动词"由……组成",可变为英语中的非谓语动词"Consisting of...",只保留"以……闻名"作谓语动词。

2. 英译中

【原文】

Without a doubt, China is one of the most adventurous countries when it comes to eating street food. There are some dishes available around which you would never consider edible in your home country. Some of them look really disgusting, but taste amazing so you should never judge Chinese food by its look.① When you come to China, be adventurous with food.

Here is my top 10 Chinese street foods you simply can't afford to miss when in China:

(1) Baozi

These are traditional Chinese dumplings. They are often steamed or fried and filled with a great voice of meat (pork, beef) and veggies (steamed peas, sweetcorn, chives, and chopped carrot). Baozi are served with soy-based sauce, chili, vinegar and sesame oil.

(2) Jiaozi

Jiaozi is also called Chinese dumpling, but crescent-shaped and much smaller than baozi. They are usually filled with minced stuffing and steamed and they are served boiled or fried.

(3) Snake meat

Snake meat is a delicacy served mainly in Guilin area, so if you make it to Li River nearby Yangshuo, you should not miss it. It's a very delicious and soft dish which tastes like perfectly grilled fish. It is mainly served with deep fried veggies.

(4) Snails and the beer

The snails, a very famous dish in Guilin, are usually served in shell and taste like a minced beef. They are cooked in beer and served with a bottle of beer as well. It's very spicy, so be careful before digging in.

(5) Duck and chicken feet

They are very spicy, but extremely delicious and convenient to pack for your train ride. They are served as a beer snack and usually deep fried, then steamed before being stewed.

(6) Stinky tofu

Stinky tofu (chòu dòufu) is a form of fermented tofu that has a strong odor. It is a snack that is usually sold at night markets or roadside stands or as a side dish.

(7) Grilled chicks

It is a vacuum-packed snack often eaten in local trains and buses. They are salt-baked or grilled. ② You might go for a spicy version or the mild one if it does not disgust you.

(8) Youtiao

It's a very common breakfast in China. Youtiao is simply deep fried bread stick made of dough and served hot as an accompaniment for rice congee or soy milk.

(9) Baked sweet potatoes

Great snack option for vegetarians. They are baked in a huge barrel in the street, extremely soft and dry so make sure you get them with soy milk or tea.

(10) Fried rice

Fried rice with vegetables and bean curd—a very common street food made by locals. The rice is served in bowls with meat and vegetables as toppings and adding some bean curd (processed from soybeans) on top will make it taste even better.

【译文】

说到吃街边小吃,中国无疑是一个最需要勇气的国家。有些小吃可能在你的国家你永远也不会去吃的。而有些小吃看上去很恶心,吃起来却特别好吃,所以千万不要仅看外表就去评判中国的食物。①既然到了中国,还是要大胆尝试各种食物。

下面是我列出的 10 种你不能错过的中国街头小吃。

(1) 包子

包子是传统的中国包馅食物,通常是蒸制或者煎制的,馅子是肉(猪肉,牛肉)和蔬菜(蒸豌豆、甜玉米、葱、胡萝卜丝)。包子一般和酱油、辣椒酱、醋以及麻油一起食用。

(2) 饺子

饺子也是种包馅食物,但是成新月形,比包子小很多,里面包的是剁碎的馅子,有蒸饺、水饺和煎饺。

(3) 蛇肉

蛇肉主要是桂林一带的美味,如果你在阳朔附近的漓江旅游,你千万不要错过这个美味。蛇肉味道鲜美,口感绵软,吃起来味道像烤鱼,一般跟炸蔬菜一起食用。

(4) 田螺和啤酒

田螺是桂林的一道名菜,通常是连壳一起炒的,吃起来味道像碎牛肉。一般是和啤酒一起烹调,吃的时候可搭配啤酒一起食用,田螺的味道有些辣,所以吃时要注意点。

(5) 鸭脚和鸡脚

非常辣但很美味,适合火车旅行时候享用,一般是作为啤酒的下酒菜,通常先用油炸一下,然后蒸,再炖。

(6) 臭豆腐

臭豆腐是一种发酵的豆腐,味道刺鼻,通常在夜市上或街边小摊上有售,或者做主菜的配菜。

(7) 烧鸡

烧鸡是真空包装的小吃,常在当地火车或者大巴上食用,通常是盐焗或者烧烤而成。②如果你觉得味道还行的话,可以来点辣的或者不辣的。

(8) 油条

这是中国常见的早点之一。油条是由面粉做的长条油炸而成,就着稀饭或者豆浆趁热吃。

(9) 烤红薯

烤红薯是素食者青睐的小吃,街边小摊贩把红薯放大桶里烤好,特别软,有点干,可以和豆浆或者茶一起食用。

(10) 炒饭

炒饭配蔬菜和豆腐,是当地常见的小吃,米饭装在碗里,上面放些肉和蔬菜,再加上点豆腐(由黄豆制成)会更加美味。

【译文分析】

①When you come to China, be adventurous with food.

译文:既然到了中国,还是要大胆尝试各种食物。

此句中的"you"是泛指,可以省略,处理成无主句。另外原句中的形容词词组"be adventurous with...",在翻译成中文时可处理为动词词组"大胆尝试"。

②You might go for a spicy version or the mild one if it does not disgust you.

译文:如果你觉得味道还行的话,可以来点辣的或者不辣的。

如果有时不好直译的话,可以正话反译,如句中的"if it does not disgust you",反过来说意思就是"如果你觉得味道还行的话"。

Ⅴ. 技能训练之记忆训练

口译记忆是口译的关键步骤,由于口语表达的速度较快,如果只是记词,只能记住几个支离破碎的词语,很容易忘记整体意思,所以听力记忆要记意而不是记词。听力的记忆练习需要延长信息在短时记忆中停留的时间,以便为信息的翻译提供机会。口译记忆训练可以分为两步,第一步先进行跟读练习,然后再进行复述练习。

1. 跟读练习

跟读练习也称影子练习,指跟读源语,要求学员在倾听源语讲话的同时,以落后于讲话人 2 至 3 秒的时差,用同一种语言将讲话内容完整准确地复述出来。随着熟练程度的提高,学员可以将时差逐渐拉大到落后于讲话人半句到一句话,从句子跟读逐步过渡到段落跟读。

2. 复述练习

复述练习包括源语和译语复述练习。先从源语复述练习开始,然后再进行译语复述。可以从句子复述开始,再慢慢过渡到段落复述,从短的段落慢慢过渡到较长的段落。无论是源语复述还是译语复述,重要的是重现意义框架,不应拘泥于字面,学员要慢慢从对源语讲话所有字词的忠实复述,改为对讲话内容的概括和综述。

请跟读和复述以下文章:

The average American eats a lot of red meat, such as beef and meat from other mammals.

Meat-eaters often note that red meat has a lot of protein, which helps repair muscles and build bones. But new research shows that if people want to live a long and healthy life, they should get their protein from plants.

Dr. Mingyang Song and Dr. Andrew Chan work at Massachusetts General Hospital and Harvard University. They and other researchers examined how proteins from animals and proteins from plants affect human health.

They examined information from two major, long-term studies. The studies gathered information about the diet, lifestyle and health of more than 130,000 people. Dr. Chan says the information showed how to live a longer and healthier life.

One important finding was that people who ate the highest amounts of animal-based protein, such as red meat, had a higher risk of dying earlier. They were especially at risk of dying earlier from heart-related problems.

One reason is that red meat has high levels of cholesterol, which has been linked to heart disease.

The researchers found that heart-related or cardiovascular-problems were higher among people who ate meat and also smoked，drank heavily，were obese and did not exercise.

While getting protein is important，red meat is not the only or best source. Dr. Chan said researchers found that people who replaced animal protein with plant protein in their diet reduced their risk of early death.

Ⅵ. 词汇拓展

开胃品 starter

色拉 salad

主菜 main course

甜点 dessert

招牌菜 house specialty

羊角面包 croissant

麦片粥 cereal

（牛排）三分熟 rare

（牛排）五分熟 medium

（牛排）全熟 well done

对……过敏 allergic

枣 Chinese date

甘蔗 sugar cane

猕猴桃 kiwi fruit/Chinese gooseberry

芹菜 celery

菠菜 spinach

蚝油 oyster sauce

饮料 beverages

茉莉花茶 jasmine tea

奶昔 milk-shake

香草冰淇淋 vanilla ice-cream

酸奶 yoghurt

伏特加酒 vodka

鸡尾酒 cocktail

浓缩果汁 concentrated juice

爱尔啤酒(美国)ale

生啤酒 draft beer

(苏格兰)大麦酒 barley-beer

薄荷糖 mint

话梅 prune candied plum

参考文献

[1] http：//wenku.baidu.com/view/b825b8eb998fcc22bcd10d0d.html.

[2] http：//etramping.com/10-chinese-street-foods-and-drinks-not-to-miss/.

[3] http：//news.163.com/10/0412/16/64386STH000146BD_4.html.

第三章 礼仪祝辞

Ⅰ. 词汇预习

Your Excellency 尊敬的陛下

Head of State 政府首脑

balmy season 宜人的季节

a heartfelt welcome 衷心的欢迎

a time-honored tradition 自古的传统

peaceful development 和平发展

win-win cooperation 合作共赢，双赢

a concerted effort 齐心协力

Ⅱ. 典型句型

1. 英译中

（1）Mr. President，Prince Philip and I are delighted to welcome you and Madame Peng to Buckingham Palace this evening.

主席先生，菲利普亲王和我本人非常高兴地欢迎您和您的夫人彭丽媛女士今晚来白金汉宫做客。

（2）Michelle and I send our warmest wishes to everyone celebrating the Lunar New Year here in America and all around the world.

米歇尔和我为全美国和全世界庆祝农历新年的人们，送上最真挚的祝福！

（3）Ladies and Gentlemen，I ask you to rise and drink a toast to the President and Madame Peng and to the people of China.

女士们，先生们，我请大家起立，共同举杯，为习近平主席和夫人彭丽媛女士的健康、为中国人民的健康与幸福，干杯！

（4）Today，we have had thorough and fruitful discussions on the meeting's theme and major topics and exchanged views on the vison of Asia-Pacific development and the future direction of APEC cooperation. As a result，we have reached extensive and important consensus.

我们今天围绕会议主题和几大议题进行了热烈而富有成效的讨论，就亚太发展愿景和亚太经合组织合作方向等问题深入交换看法，达成了许多重要共识。

（5）In conclusion，I wish the forum full success and all the guests coming from afar and friends attending the conference a fruitful and enjoyable stay here and good health.

最后，预祝本届年会取得圆满成功！祝远道而来的各位嘉宾和与会的各位朋友工作顺利、生活愉快、身体健康！

2. 中译英

（1）我很高兴和我的同事、商务部部长高虎城先生作为会议联合主席，主持今天的会议。

It gives me great pleasure to co-chair this meeting with my colleague，Minister of Commerce Gao Hucheng.

（2）借此机会，我谨向各位企业家朋友，以及长期为促进中爱友好合作做出积极贡献的各界人士，表示衷心的感谢，并致以良好的祝愿！

I would like to take this opportunity to express heartfelt thanks and extend best wishes to the business leaders present today and all those who have contributed to China-Ireland friendship and cooperation over the year.

（3）在我正式宣布会议结束之前，我想借此机会向各位同事表示诚挚谢意。感谢你们对我本人和中国政府的信任，感谢你们在会议期间给予中方的支持、理解、合作，感谢你们对亚太共同发展、繁荣、进步事业的辛勤努力和付出。

Before I officially close our meeting，I wish to take this opportunity to express my sincere thanks to you all for the trust you have placed in me and the Chinese government. I thank you for your support，understanding and cooperation during the meeting and for your dedication and contribution to the common development，prosperity and progress of the Asia-Pacific.

（4）我相信，这样一个无限光明、无限美好的明天，必将到来！

I am convinced that such an immensely bright and beautiful tomorrow will arrive!

（5）我希望这次中国之行能给大家留下美好的回忆，也借此次机会祝大家旅途愉快，一路平安！

I hope you have enjoyed your stay in China，and wish you all a pleasant and safe trip!

Ⅲ. 段落翻译

1. 中译英

【原文】

尊敬的各位元首、政府首脑、议长、国际组织负责人、部长,博鳌亚洲论坛理事会各位成员,各位来宾,女士们,先生们,朋友们:

椰风暖人,海阔天高。在这美好的季节里,同大家相聚在美丽的海南岛,参加博鳌亚洲论坛2013年会,我感到十分高兴。首先,我谨代表中国政府和人民,并以我个人的名义,向各位朋友的到来,表示诚挚的欢迎! 对年会的召开,表示热烈的祝贺!

……

亲仁善邻,是中国自古以来的传统。亚洲和世界和平发展、合作共赢的事业没有终点,只有一个接一个的新起点。中国愿同五大洲的朋友们携手努力,共同创造亚洲和世界的美好未来,造福亚洲和世界人民!

最后,预祝年会取得圆满成功!

【译文】

Your Excellencies, Heads of State and Government, Speakers of Parliament, Heads of International Organizations, Ministers, Members of the Board of Directors of the Bo'ao Forum for Asia, Distinguished Guests, Ladies and Gentlemen, Dear Friends,

In this balmy season with clear sky and warm, coconut-scented breeze, I am so glad to meet all of you at the Annual Conference 2013 of the Bo'ao Forum for Asia here in Hainan, a picturesque island embraced by the vast ocean. Let me begin by extending, on behalf of the Chinese government and people and also in my own name, a heartfelt welcome to you and warm congratulations on the opening of the Annual Conference of the Bo'ao Forum.

...

Promoting good neighborliness is a time-honored tradition of China. To enhance peaceful development and win-win cooperation in Asia and the world is a race that has one starting point after another and knows no finishing line. We in China are ready to join hands with friends from across the world in a concerted effort to create a bright future for both Asia and the world and bring benefit to the Asian people and the people around the world.

In conclusion, I wish the Bo, ao Forum for Asia Annual Conference 2013 every success!

2. 英译中

【原文】

I wish to extend warm congratulations on the opening of the fifth Annual Meeting of the Summer Davos, and a sincere welcome to you all. It's been five years since the launch of the Summer Davos. In these five years, the Summer Davos has set a clear objective for itself, that is, it is a forum for the world, for the future, for innovation and for the youth. The diverse forms of discussions conducted during the forum are lively and vibrant. In particular, during the difficult times of the financial crisis, the forum sent out a message of hope and brought confidence and courage to the world. The theme of this year's forum—Mastering Quality Growth—represents people's shared desire for robust, sustainable and balanced economic growth, and I wish the meeting a great success.

【译文】

我对第五届夏季达沃斯论坛的召开表示衷心祝贺！对各位嘉宾的到来表示热烈欢迎！夏季达沃斯论坛已经走过了五个年头,五年的论坛形成了一个宗旨,这就是面向世界、面向未来、面向创新、面向青年。会议安排了多种形式的讨论,开得生动活泼、充满朝气,特别在金融危机的困难时期,给世界传递了希望的声音,带来了信心和勇气。本次论坛以"关注增长质量,掌控经济格局"为主题,反映了大家对推动经济强劲、可持续、平衡增长的共识与期待。我祝愿本次论坛获得圆满成功!

IV. 篇章翻译

1. 中译英

【原文】

首先,请允许我代表中国外交部对出席今晚招待会的各位贵宾表示热烈欢迎。

20 年前,怀着连接亚欧大陆两端、促进亚欧稳定繁荣的愿望,亚欧 26 方领导人聚首泰国曼谷,举行第一届亚欧首脑会议,确立了建设亚欧新型全面伙伴关系的共同目标,开启了亚欧全方位对话合作的新的航程。

20 年间,亚欧合作不断拓展深入。我们定期开展政治对话,增进了相互了解和信任;我们不断拓展经贸联系,实现了亚欧经济增长和可持续发展;我们就气候变化、恐怖主义等全球性挑战加强合作,彰显了多边主义的有效性;我们积极开展不同文化与文明间的对话,加深了各国人民之间的友谊与感情。我们应该为亚欧会议取得的成绩感到骄傲!

①展望未来,亚欧各方应该同心协力,确保政治对话、经贸合作、人文交流这三大支

柱相互促进、平衡发展。能否加大投入、以务实合作造福各国人民将在很大程度上决定着亚欧会议的未来成败。当前尤其要做好两方面工作。

一是努力重启经贸合作进程。亚欧经济部长会议停滞十年，令人遗憾。在当前全球经济增长乏力的背景下，亚欧经贸合作需要开拓思路，深挖潜力。希望各方加紧协调，早日恢复举办这一重要部长级会议。

二是推动互联互通合作取得可见成果。将互联互通合作主流化是亚欧各方领导人的共识。各方应积极落实，加紧发展战略对接，以实实在在的成果早日造福各国人民。②充分发挥工商界、媒体和智库的能动性，为亚欧合作汇聚更多智慧和力量。

女士们，先生们，朋友们，

亚欧会议成立20年来，逐渐形成了以相互尊重、平等相待、协商一致、互不干涉内政等为基础的亚欧方式。大小国家一律平等，大事小情商量着办，成为亚欧会议保持生命力的法宝，值得我们珍惜和发扬。

中国是亚欧会议创始成员，是亚欧合作的坚定支持者和参与者。中国正在积极推进结构改革，加快新旧动能转换，实现创新驱动发展。中国在谋求大发展的进程中，将继续与亚欧各方加强合作，为亚欧乃至世界的稳定繁荣共同努力。

今年7月，第十一届亚欧首脑会议将在蒙古乌兰巴托举行。中国愿与各方携手合作，把握机遇，为亚欧会议下一个十年的更大发展做出贡献。

最后，我提议，为亚欧会议的更好发展、为亚欧人民的友好合作、为各位嘉宾的健康平安，干杯！

【译文】

First of all, please allow me to extend on behalf of the Chinese Ministry of Foreign Affairs a warm welcome to you all.

Two decades ago, with the vision of connecting and promoting stability and prosperity in Asia and Europe, leaders from 26 parties in Asia and Europe gathered in Bangkok, Thailand for the first summit of the Asia-Europe Meeting (ASEM), establishing the common goal of the new ASEM comprehensive partnership and setting out on a new journey of comprehensive dialogue and cooperation between Asia and Europe.

Over the past 20 years, Asia-Europe cooperation has kept expanding and deepening. Our regular political dialogues have enhanced mutual understanding and trust. Our expanded trade and economic links have boosted economic growth and sustainable development in Asia and Europe. We have strengthened cooperation on tackling such global challenges as climate change and terrorism, which demonstrates the effectiveness of multilateralism. And we have carried out dialogues among cultures and civilizations to deepen the friendship and affection among people of all countries. There is every reason for us to be proud of the achievements of ASEM.

①Looking ahead, countries in Asia and Europe need to make concerted efforts to ensure mutual reinforcement and balanced development of the three pillars of political dialogue, economic cooperation, and people-to-people and cultural exchanges. Whether or not efforts can be made to step up input and benefit people of all countries with practical cooperation will to a large extent determine the future success of ASEM. In particular, we should focus on the following two aspects.

First, we need to make efforts to restore the process of economic and trade cooperation. The decade-long standstill of ASEM Economic Ministers' Meeting is truly regrettable. Given the weak global economic growth, efforts should be made to foster new ideas and further unlock potential to advance the Asia-Europe trade and economic cooperation process. We hope all parties will accelerate coordination for the early resumption of this important ministerial meeting.

Second, we need to work for visible outcomes of connectivity cooperation. Mainstreaming of connectivity cooperation is a consensus among leaders from all countries in Asia and Europe. It is imperative to actively implement this consensus, build up strategic synergy, and bring tangible benefits to people of all countries at an early date. ②We need to fully mobilize the incentives of the business community, media and think-tanks to pool more wisdom and strength for Asia-Europe cooperation.

Ladies and Gentlemen, Dear Friends,

Over the past two decades since the founding of ASEM, the ASEM way based on mutual respect, equality, consensus and non-intervention in each other's internal affairs has been gradually developed. Countries, big or small, are all equals, and issues, big or small, should be settled through consultation. This principle has been crucial to the vitality of ASEM, and we should cherish it and carry it forward.

As a founding member of ASEM, China firmly supports and actively participates in Asia-Europe cooperation. China is actively promoting structural reforms, accelerating the shift from old growth drivers to new ones and pursuing innovation-driven development. When pursuing its own development, China will continue to work with all countries to strengthen cooperation between Asia and Europe and contribute to the stability and prosperity of Asia and Europe and the world at large.

The 11th ASEM Summit will be held in Ulaanbaatar, Mongolia this July. China is ready to work with other parties to seize opportunities and contribute to the greater development of ASEM in the next decade.

With that，I wish to propose a toast：

To greater development of ASEM；

To the friendship and cooperation of people in Asia and Europe；

To the health of all our guests.

Cheers!

【译文分析】

①展望未来,亚欧各方应该同心协力,确保政治对话、经贸合作、人文交流这三大支柱相互促进、平衡发展。

译文：Looking ahead，countries in Asia and Europe need to make concerted efforts to ensure mutual reinforcement and balanced development of the three pillars of political dialogue，economic cooperation，and people-to-people and cultural exchanges.

在口译过程中,要充分考虑句子主句和副句之间的所属关系,该句中"亚欧各方"为引导主句的主语,在宾语部分注意保持并列关系的词性平衡。这个句子比较巧妙地译"支柱"为"pillar"。

②充分发挥工商界、媒体和智库的能动性,为亚欧合作汇聚更多智慧和力量。

译文：We need to fully mobilize the incentives of the business community，media and think-tanks to pool more wisdom and strength for Asia-Europe cooperation.

中文句子常常出现没有主语的情况,译者要视情况添加以保持句子的完整。"智库"是近些年出现的新词,要注意掌握,译为"think-tank"。

2. 英译中

【原文】

First of all，let me thank you for coming today to the launch of "My Dream" Tour of Australia by the China Disabled People's Performing Art Troupe. I hope the short video of the performance has given you a taste of what we are launching.

This is not the first time Chinese art performances have come to Australia. We are giving special attention to this troupe due to its unique nature. I fully agree with what was said earlier by my Telstra friend，that disability is not inability.

In 2002，I had an opportunity to watch a performance by this troupe in China and I was stunned by their performance. ①It made me wonder whether music can only be appreciated by listening，whether colors can be understood by vision and whether light can be felt in a world of darkness.

The performance of "My Dream" opens a window to another world，in which a group of people, who, though, different from us in one way or another, can artistically interpret their dreams in a marvelous way. So, I am very pleased today to launch this program together with Telstra.

We are grateful for Telstra's generosity in sponsoring the troupe's Australian tour, and I would also like to thank ACBC and Air China for their contributions to the tour. Our appreciation also goes to Westpac and Bing Lee for their sponsorship for the Sydney show. I need to mention here that this tour is strongly supported by the disabled community here in Australia as well as by the federal and state governments.

This art troupe has been highly regarded in China since its founding 18 years ago. Many of the performers have won national rewards and have achieved their artistic level after going through very hard training and overcoming many difficulties. Every artist in the troupe has a story behind his success, which only goes to highlight the life and fight of the 60 million disabled people in China.

China, as a developing country, is confronted with many challenges. One of them is to improve the conditions of the disabled and provide them with equal social opportunities. ② The activities of this art troupe not only offer the Chinese people high-level artistic enjoyment, but also play an important role in gathering support for the troupe's cause in the country.

Currently, China is carrying out a nationwide debate on the amendment of the *Law on the Protection of Disabled Persons*. Many people have advanced suggestions about how to better safeguard the rights and interests of this community. We are also undertaking a national survey on the disabled community to understand their exact number, geographical distribution, causes of disability, living conditions, rehabilitation, education, employment, and so on.

The first survey was done in 1987 based on which many improvements were made. However, there have been many changes since then and it is necessary for us to consider new measures to make new improvements.

Here in Australia, you have three million people in the disabled community who enjoy good social support. For example, I noticed that in every public place, there are aids for the disabled, ranging from textured paths to ramps. There is also great support in terms of law and regulations against job discrimination. I believe there is a lot we can learn from Australia in this area.

The objectivity of the art troupe's tour of Australia are firstly, to offer an excellent Oriental art show to the people and enhance their awareness of the talents of disabled people; secondly, to promote understanding amongst the Australian people about China and the Chinese people; thirdly, to carry out exchanges with the Australian disabled community and learn from each other's experiences.

The tour will last from 24 September through 8 October. The troupe will be giving seven or eight performance in Sydney, Canberra, Brisbane, Adelaide, Melbourne, and Perth.

Today, we want to announce their tour to you and through you to the Australian public. I can assure you and everyone who attends the show that you will never forget it.

Thank you.

【译文】

首先,我要感谢各位参加今天的中国残疾人艺术团"我的梦"澳大利亚巡演新闻发布会。希望前面播放的短片已经使大家对我们所推介的演出有了大概的了解。

中国各类艺术团来澳大利亚演出不是第一次了,但是我们对此次演出给予特别关注,因为这个艺术团不同寻常。我完全同意澳大利亚电讯公司的朋友刚才所说的,残疾并不意味着能力的残缺。

2002年,我在中国有机会观看这个艺术团的演出,被他们的表演深深感动。①我感叹:难道音乐只能通过听觉来感受?难道色彩只能通过视觉来理解?难道黑暗的世界里真的无法体会到光明?

"我的梦"打开了通往另一个世界的一扇窗,让我们了解到艺术团演员们的内心。虽然他们与我们有这样或那样的不同,但仍然能够以艺术方式诠释自己的梦想,令人不可思议。所以,我今天非常高兴与澳大利亚电讯公司一道举办这个推介活动。

我要感谢澳大利亚电讯公司对艺术团澳大利亚巡演给予的大力赞助,感谢澳大利亚中国工商业委员会和中国国际航空公司的支持,也要感谢澳大利亚西太银行和并立电器对此次悉尼演出的赞助。这里我还要特别提到,此次演出得到了澳大利亚残疾人团体和联邦、州政府的大力支持。

中国残疾人艺术团成立于18年前,在中国享有盛誉,许多演员都获得过国家级奖项,他们经过艰苦训练、克服了许多困难才达到这样的艺术水平。艺术团每个演员成功的背后都有一个故事,他们是中国6000多万残疾人顽强生活和奋斗的代表。

中国作为一个发展中国家,面临着很多挑战,其中之一就是改善残疾人的生活状况,为他们提供平等的社会机会。②残疾人艺术团在中国不仅为人民带来高水平的艺术享受,也为赢得社会对残疾人事业的支持发挥了重要作用。

目前,中国正在就修改《残疾人保障法》展开全国性的讨论,社会各界提出了许多更好地保障残疾人权益的意见。我们还在对残疾人进行全国普查,主要是调查具体人数、分布、致残原因、生活条件、康复、教育和就业等情况。

第一次普查是1987年完成的,在此基础上做了很多改进工作。但是过去的十多年中国发生了很多变化,我们必须考虑采取新的措施进一步改善残疾人的状况。

澳大利亚有300万残疾人,他们享有非常好的社会支持。例如,我注意到在每个公共场所都有方便残疾人的盲道和坡道等。再比如,你们在法律法规上有多种措施避免对残疾人的就业歧视等。我认为,在这个领域,中国有很多方面可以向澳大利亚学习。

此次艺术团来访的主要目的:一是向大家献上精彩的东方艺术,让人们了解残疾人的才艺;二是促进澳大利亚人民对中国和中国人民的了解;三是与澳大利亚残疾人进行交流,相互学习。

此次巡演将于9月24日开始,直到10月8日结束。艺术团将在悉尼、堪培拉、布里斯班、阿德莱德、墨尔本和珀斯进行七至八场演出。

今天,我们要向你们——并且通过你们——向澳大利亚公众宣布残疾人艺术团的巡演。我保证,每一位观众都会对演出终身难忘。

谢谢。

【译文分析】

①It made me wonder whether music can only be appreciated by listening, whether colors can be understood by vision and whether light can be felt in a world of darkness.

译文:我感叹:难道音乐只能通过听觉来感受?难道色彩只能通过视觉来理解?难道黑暗的世界里真的无法体会到光明?

口译过程中尽量考虑口语习惯,将形式主语"it"转换。译者将间接引语译为反问句,在句式上的叠加让语气更加丰富。

②The activities of this art troupe not only offer the Chinese people high-level artistic enjoyment, but also play an important role in gathering support for the troupe's cause in the country.

译文:残疾人艺术团在中国不仅为人民带来高水平的艺术享受,也为赢得社会对残疾人事业的支持发挥了重要作用。

"not only...but also…"并列句式在英文中是常见的句型,通常译为"不但……而且……"或者"不仅……也……"。

Ⅴ.技能训练之笔记训练

笔记技巧是帮助译员完成口译的重要辅助手段之一,但是口译笔记不等同于速记,并不是单独的一门学科,仅仅只是一个技巧,除开一些通用符号之外,口译笔记纯粹是译员个人的记忆方式展示。

速记是对说话者的原话记录,作为口头材料的忠实记录转化成书面记录,常适用于会议记录和法庭记录等场合,而速记员也是一种职业。口译笔记不同,是作为译员口译过程中的协助记忆方式存在,尤其是在做长交传过程中,说话人篇幅过长,则译员需要记录一些重要信息以免遗漏。恰当的笔记可以帮助译员回顾信息,以免因为大脑疲劳等问题造成记忆流失。

口译笔记要求简单、明了、准确,但同时有个性化特征,因为译员的记录方式不同且存在暂时性。口译笔记的详略应以现场要求为准,不应一味求简,也不应一味求细,而是在不同要求之下随机应变,作为记忆的补充。

通常口译笔记记录下来的方式并没有定式,可以为母语+符号,也可以目标语+母语+符号,一切以译员习惯为标准,以能帮助译员完成口译任务为目的。好的译员会不断训练自己,优化笔记方式,帮助提高口译质量。

常用的完成口译笔记过程要遵循如下标准。

1. 工具简单

口译过程中常常使用的上下翻动的小型活页记事本,纸张质量要好,行距要宽,易翻动。记录过程中为从上至下的纵向记录。使用记录的笔要流畅,常用圆珠笔,因其使用寿命相比水笔更长。有经验的译员会有备用的记事本和记录笔。

2. 意群独立

笔记过程中要划分意群,一般用斜线隔开,对于不同篇幅的材料可以采用单斜线或者双斜线方式隔开,然后另起一行,避免信息太多,影响视力范围。

3. 结构明确

笔记内容要能区分结构,不要造成串行,不要有插入标示,否则容易引起混淆,要养成习惯,在每个节点结束之后做好标示,能清楚知道层次,可以在一个框架之下画上一道横线,表示一段的完成。

要掌握常用的笔记符号方式,如下:

发展 ↗	减少 ↘
上升 ↑	下降 ↓
认同 √	回顾 ←
展望 →	反对 ×

音乐♪	大于＞
小于＜	等于＝
约等于≈	大于等于≥
小于等于≤	左右之间±
增加＋	减少—
包含{	引用""
更好＋＋	更差－－
因为∵	所以∴
摄氏度℃	华氏度℉
百分比%	千分比‰
问题?	惊叹!
和 &	对立冲突＞＜
同意 Y	不同意 N
人民币¥	美元 $
欧元€	英镑£
高兴:)	忧伤:(
优秀☆	at@
to 2	for 4
and &	against vs

口译笔记使用的原则是帮助译员完成口译任务,不宜过分追求美感和独特性,需要反复练习使用,以辅助完成译员口译任务为目的。译员要谨记,笔记是服务于口译的,不要受限于笔记的数量,在不同的场合,听懂说话人的意图,再结合笔记的帮助,才能达成口译的效果要求。

提供一个笔记范文供学习者参考。

【范文】

在本轮对话中,希望双方再接再厉,共同努力,既立足当前,又着眼长远,推动中美战略与经济对话成为两国加强战略沟通、增进战略互信、促进战略合作的长效机制,为建设中美合作伙伴关系不断进行探索和实践。

【笔记】

/T,2方/希,{接＋厉}

(S＋L

→中美{S＋E} T

→2 SC＋ST＋SC 长机

→2 P R {探＋实}//

Ⅵ. 词汇拓展

贵宾 honorable guest

尊贵的朋友 esteemed company

高层领导人 senior leader

使节 diplomatic envoy

大会 assembly

论坛 forum

宴会 banquet

告别会 farewell party

博览会 exposition

茶会 tea party

招待会 reception

代表大会 congress

全会 plenum

研讨会 symposium

分会 session

圆桌会议 roundtable

座谈会 panel

联欢会 gala

董事会 board of directors

鸡尾酒会 cocktail party

自助餐会 buffet party

午餐会 luncheon meeting

行业展览会 trade show

签字仪式 signing ceremony

毕业典礼 commencement ceremony

揭幕式 unveiling ceremony

开学典礼 new term ceremony

很荣幸…… It is a great privilege to...

宣布开幕 declare...open

宣布闭幕 declare the closing of...

承蒙……的诚挚邀请 at the gracious invitation of...

谨代表 on behalf of

为表达我对……的感谢 express my gratitude to...

表达我对……最热烈的祝贺 send my warmest congratulations to...

重要时刻 momentous time

富有成效的讨论 fruitful discussions

荣辱与共 share weal and woe

新未来 new vistas

共识 consensus

重大承诺 major commitment

迎新年 usher in the new year

辞旧岁 bid farewell to the old year

展望未来 look ahead

民族复兴 national renewal

与时俱进 keep pace with the times

发展新动能 new driver of growth

质量强国 a country strong on quality

中国特色大国外交理念

the philosophy underpinning China's diplomacy as a major country

为政之道,民生为本。

That government is best which gives prime place to the wellbeing of the people.

简除烦苛,禁察非法。

Cut red tape and root out illegalities.

上下同欲者胜。

Success comes to those who share in one purpose.

国际产能合作

international cooperation on production capacity

全面建成小康社会决胜阶段

the decisive stage in finishing building a moderately prosperous society in all respects

物质文明和精神文明协调发展

ensure that cultural-ethical and material development progress together

经济建设和国防建设融合发展

integrated development of the economy and national defense

引领中国经济发展新常态

guide the new normal in China's economic development

协调是持续健康发展的内在要求。

Coordination is an integral aspect of sustained and healthy development.

绿色是永续发展的必要条件和人民对美好生活追求的重要体现。

Green，which represents an eco-friendly outlook，is a necessary condition for ensuring lasting development as well as an important way in which people pursue a better life.

开放是中国繁荣发展的必由之路。

Opening-up is the path China must take to achieve prosperity and development.

共享是中国特色社会主义的本质要求。

Sharing is the essence of socialism with Chinese characteristics.

我们对你们的到来表示热烈的欢迎！

We wish to extend a warm welcome to all of you.

祝大会圆满成功！

To wish the conference much success!

参考文献

［1］傅莹. 在彼处：大使演讲录［M］. 北京：外语教学与研究出版社，2012.

［2］王学文. 口译实训［M］. 北京：外文出版社，2015.

［3］http：//www.fmprc.gov.cn/web/.

［4］http：//www.chinadaily.com.cn/.

第四章 旅游观光

I. 词汇预习

landmark 地标

expand 延伸

commemorate 纪念

exceptional beauty 不同寻常的美丽

climatic zone 气候带

uninhabited area 无人居住的区域

astonishing variety 令人惊叹的不同形态

II. 典型句型

1. 英译中

（1）Gulangyu Island，a small island in southwestern Xiamen，covers an area of 1.78 square kilometers，and is known as "the Garden on the Sea". It is surrounded by the sea，and has beautiful landscape. It is listed as one of the state-level scenic spots.

鼓浪屿是位于厦门西南隅的一个小岛，面积仅 1.78 平方千米，素以"海上花园"的美称享誉中外，是国家级重点风景名胜区。

（2）Xi'an，the capital of Shaanxi Province，is a new industrial base and scientific and educational center in China. It is the hub of communications between eastern and western China and is an important city in Northwest China.

西安是陕西省的省会，是我国新兴的工业基地和科教中心城市，也是中国东西交通的枢纽和西北地区重要的城市。

（3）Travel and tourism between our countries is crucial to build stronger cultural and economic ties. This generates greater understanding and friendship between our people. And it also generates greater prosperity.

我们两国之间的旅游业对于建设更为牢固的文化与经济纽带十分重要,它能增进两国人民之间的了解与友谊,并能促进经济繁荣。

(4) The tourism year was announced by President Xi Jinping and US President Barack Obama during Xi's state visit to the United States in September.

旅游年活动是去年9月中国国家主席习近平在访问美国时,和美国总统奥巴马共同提出的。

(5) It's an effective way to deepen the understanding and friendship between the two peoples and an important source to boost bilateral economic and trade cooperation.

它是深化两国文化交流、增进人民友谊的有效方式,也是促进双边经贸合作的重要源头。

2. 中译英

(1) 举办这样的展览的意义在于向全世界展示我国敦煌艺术的精华,让全世界的人民都来了解中华民族的优秀文化。

The significance of such exhibition was to show the world the cream of Dunhuang art so as to enable the people of the world to understand the excellent cultural heritage of the Chinese nation.

(2) 这座寺庙历史悠久,可追溯到初唐时期。

The temple has a long history dating back to the early period of the Tang Dynasty.

(3) 该城市有全国规模最大、最负盛名的园林。

The city boasts the largest and the most famous garden in the country.

(4) 到2020年,构建起由自然资源资产产权制度、国土空间开发保护制度等八项制度构成的生态文明制度体系。

By 2020, an institutional framework composed of eight systems will have been established for promoting ecological progress, including a property rights system for natural resource assets and a system for developing and protecting territorial space.

(5) 紧紧围绕建设美丽中国,深化生态文明体制改革,加快建立生态文明制度,推动形成人与自然和谐发展现代化建设新格局。

To build a beautiful China, we will deepen reform to promote ecological progress and move faster to establish related systems so as to create a new model of modernization that ensures humanity develops in harmony with nature.

Ⅲ. 段落翻译

1. 中译英

【原文】

天安门，作为皇城的正门入口，长期以来就是北京的地标。广场南面是在 1919 年五四运动期间作为历史上反对帝国主义游行的地点，而五四运动是新文化运动的重要部分。1949 年中华人民共和国成立以后，广场面积扩大到 40 公顷，是原来的好几倍，成为世界上最大的城市中心广场。广场中央矗立着为纪念那些为革命献身的英雄而修建的人民英雄纪念碑，广场最南端是毛泽东纪念堂。

【译文】

Tian'anmen(Gate of Heavenly Peace)，the front entrance of the Imperial City，has long been a landmark of Beijing. The square to its south was the scene of historic anti-imperialist demonstrations during the May 4th Movement of 1919，which were a major part of a campaign for a new cultural. Since the founding of the P.R.C. in 1949，the square was expanded to cover 40 hectares，several times its original size and became the largest such square in any city in the world. In the center of the square stands the Monument to the Heroes of the people，a structure built to commemorate those who gave up their lives for the revolution，and at the southern end of the square is Mao Zedong Memorial Hall.

2. 英译中

【原文】

Australia is a land of exceptional beauty. It is the world's smallest continent and largest island，a relatively young nation established in an ancient land. A series of geological and historical accidents have made Australia one of the world's most attractive countries from the tourist's viewpoint. This country has a land area of 7,686,850 square kilometers and its coastline is 36,735 kilometers. The vast movements of the earth's crust created a vast land of Australia，isolated it and positioned it across the tropical and temperate climatic zone. Here you witness an astonishing variety of environments，from desert to rain forest，from tropical beach to white snowfield，from big，sophisticated cities to vast uninhabited areas.

【译文】

澳大利亚是一个异常美丽的国家。这是世界上最小的洲，也是最大的岛，是在古老的土地上建立起来的较为年轻的国家。地质史上，这块土地的地貌形态发生了一系列变化,澳大利亚在旅游者眼中成了世界上最吸引人的国家之一。这个国家的陆地面积为7686850平方千米,海岸线长达36 735千米。剧烈的地壳运动使澳大利亚成了幅员辽阔,与大陆分离,地处温、热带地区的国家。游客在澳大利亚可以观赏到各种地形风貌,从沙漠到热带雨林,从地处热带的海滩到白雪皑皑的田野,从扑朔迷离的大都市到人迹罕至的旷野。景观各异,令人叹为观止。

Ⅳ. 篇章翻译

1. 英译中

【原文】

San Francisco, open your Golden Gate, sang the girl in the theatre. She never finished her song. The date was 18th April, 1906. The earth shook and the roof suddenly divided, buildings crashed to the ground and people rushed out into the streets. The dreadful earthquake destroyed the city that had grown up when men discovered gold in the deserts of California. But today the streets of San Francisco stretch over more than forty steep hills, rising like huge cliffs above the blue waters of the Pacific Ocean.

The best way to see this splendid city, where Spanish people were the first to make their homes, is to take one of the old cable cars which run along the nine main avenues.① Fares are cheap; they have not risen, I'm told, for almost a hundred years.

You leave the palm trees in Union Square—the heart of San Francisco—and from the shop signs and the faces around you, you will notice that in the city live people from many nations—Austrians, Italians, Chinese and others—giving each part a special character. More Chinese live in China Town than in any other part of the world outside China. Here, with Chinese restaurants, Chinese post-boxes, and even odd telephone-boxes that look like pagodas, it is easy to feel you are in China itself.

Fisherman's Wharf, a place all foreigners want to see, is at the end of the ride. You get out, pause perhaps to help the other travelers to swing the cable car on its turntable (a city custom), and then set out to find a table in one of the gay little restaurants beside the harbor. As you enjoy the fresh Pacific sea food you can admire the bright red paint of the Golden Gate Bridge in the harbor and watch the traffic crossing beneath the tall towers on its way to the pretty village of Tiberon. When you've finished your meal, you may decide to take a boat-trip around the bay to look at the sights. You can stare, for example, at the famous, now empty, prison of

Alcatraz. Then why not go to the fishing village of Sausalito—a little like London's Chelsea or New York's Greenwich Village—to see people painting and to look at their pictures. You will be able to enjoy a view of the city from the sea and take pleasure in the soft red and blue Spanish-type houses shining in the bright Pacific light. If you have time, you might like to go by bus to Carmel, a hundred miles south of San Francisco, where you will discover a wild and wonderful coast with high cliffs.

Although the people of San Francisco prefer riding to walking, you may like to climb up the steep streets. Handrails are provided so that you can pull yourself up. You can enjoy the splendid shops, the view from Telegraph Hill, the houses with fountains and garden. You can also look at the Stage Coach, a familiar sight from Western films, which is in the window of the Wells Fargo Bank in Montgomery Street, near the business center of the city.

②I expect you'll notice that all over the city the cars are left with their wheels being turned towards the sidewalk so that they can't roll away. Wherever you walk you'll find it hard to lose yourself. At most of the important crossings there is a plan of the streets (Lombard Street; Ohio Street; Market Street; and so on)cut into the stone of the sidewalk so that you can look down and see where you are.

After so much walking you may feel tired and sticky and ready for a swim. There is often a thick morning mist from the sea in summer, but the weather can be very hot. Yet nobody swims in the Pacific. It is too risky. There are miles and miles of smooth hard sand, empty because of sharks—those dreadful big man-eating fish—and the high and dangerous waves of the sea. So take a street car from the city center to the wonderful swimming pool on the edge of the ocean. Afterwards you can go to the neighboring zoo. Later, while you wait to catch a street car returning to your hotel, you may even see the sign "Doggy Diner"—a restaurant for dogs!

But what about meals for people? As in most of the big cities, the restaurants offer delicious food from almost every country. You could have dinner in Chinatown and then, on the way back to your hotel, catch the last cable car after midnight; it's not unusual for passengers who arrive late to have to hang on to the sides of the last car for the whole journey.

On Sundays parents often take their children to look at the strange trees in the pretty Japanese Tea Garden in the huge spaces of Golden Gate Park.

With its hot sun and gay night life, San Francisco is a fine place to live in or to visit. It is the most European of all American cities and you'll be sure to grow fond of it instantly. So tell yourself in the words of a song from the last century, "San Francisco, here I come!"

【译文】

"旧金山,敞开你的金门吧!"剧院里的那位歌女演唱道。她没有唱完她的歌。这一天是 1906 年 4 月 18 日,大地震动,屋顶突然分裂,高楼大厦轰然坍倒,人们纷纷从屋里逃出,冲上街头。在加利福尼亚州沙漠里发现金矿后成长起来的这座城市,就这样被可怕的地震摧毁了。但时至今日,旧金山的街道四处延伸,遍布四十多座陡峭的小山,那些小山像悬崖峭壁般高耸于太平洋蓝色的海域之上。

要游览这座西班牙人最早在此落户的灿烂的城市,最好的办法是乘坐穿越九条主要大街的旧式缆车。①缆车收费低廉,据说近百年来一直没涨过价。

联合广场是旧金山的中心,如果你离开广场的棕榈树,你就会根据店铺的招牌和周围人们的脸庞,注意到这座城市里居住着来自许多国家的人——奥地利人、意大利人、中国人和其他国家的人——这就使每一地段呈现出各自的特色。有许多中国人住在唐人街,其人数比中国本土之外世界其他任何地方的华人都多。这里有中国风味的餐馆、中国式的邮筒,甚至还有形如宝塔的奇异的电话亭。这种景象使你很容易感到仿佛是置身于中国境内了。

国外游客都想访问一下缆车的终点站——渔人码头。车抵终点站,你下车后,也可能会暂时停步,遵照当地的风俗,帮助其他游客推动转车台上的缆车,使之掉头转向,然后移步到码头旁边的一家装饰华丽的小饭馆里找一个座位坐下。当你品尝太平洋的海鲜时,你可以观赏海港里漆着鲜红颜色的金门大桥,观看林立的高塔下通往美丽的村庄蒂伯龙的交通线上络绎不绝的车辆。餐后,你可能决定乘坐游艇绕着海湾观赏风景。比如你可以凝视遐迩闻名但现已空无一人的阿尔卡特拉兹监狱。接着,你何不去游玩一下桑萨利托渔村呢?那里有点像伦敦的切尔西区,也有些像纽约的格林威治村。有些人在渔村里绘画,你不妨去看看,观赏一下他们的作品。那时你还可以从海上远眺市容,饱览在太平洋上明媚的阳光照耀下闪闪发光的色调柔和、红蓝色的西班牙式房屋。如果有时间,你也许还想坐公共汽车前往旧金山以南一百英里的卡梅尔。在那里你会发现一片峭壁高耸、荒凉、但引人入胜的海岸。

虽然旧金山人喜欢乘车代步,可是你也许会喜欢爬坡度很大的街道。你可以抓住栏杆攀登,欣赏那些绚丽多彩的店铺,从电报山上眺望美景,饱览带有喷泉和花园的住宅。你还可以去看看陈列在韦尔斯法戈银行橱窗里的、在西部电影里常见的驿站马车,这家银行坐落在靠近城市商业中心的蒙哥马利大街。

②我想你会注意到,全市的汽车在停靠时为了防止滑动,车轮总是向着人行道的。还有,你无论走到哪里,都不容易迷路。在大多数的主要交叉路口,都有一幅街道(朗巴德街、俄亥俄街、市场街等等)的详图刻在人行道的石头上。只要你低头看一下,就知道

自己所在的位置了。

长时间走动之后，你可能感到疲倦，很不舒服，想要游泳。这里的夏季清晨，海上往往吹来浓雾，但气候可能十分炎热。然而，谁也不敢在太平洋里游泳。那样太危险了。海边有连绵数英里长的平坦坚硬的沙滩，渺无人迹，因为那里有吃人的凶猛可怕的大鲨鱼，还有海上卷起的汹涌巨浪。所以你还是从中心乘电车到太平洋岸边出色的游泳池去吧。之后，你可以逛一下附近的动物园。接着，在你等候电车回旅舍的时候，还可能会看到"狗饭店"的招牌——一家专门为狗服务的餐馆！

可是供应旅客的饭菜是什么呢？这里的餐馆和大多数大城市的餐馆一样，世界各国的美味佳肴几乎应有尽有。你不妨在唐人街就餐，饭后赶午夜以后的末班缆车返回旅舍，晚到的乘客常常不得不抓着末班缆车的车侧走完全程。

每逢星期天，家长们往往带着孩子去参观金门公园占很大面积的美丽的日本茶场，观赏茶场里那些稀奇古怪的树木。

旧金山白天骄阳当空，夜生活热闹繁华，是个适宜于居住和旅游的好地方。它是美国所有城市中最富欧洲色彩的一个城市，你肯定会很快就会喜爱它的。因此请你默念19世纪一首歌曲中这样的词句吧："旧金山，我到你的身边来了！"

【译文分析】

①Fares are cheap；they have not risen，I'm told，for almost a hundred years.

译文：缆车收费低廉，据说近百年来一直没涨过价。

插入语的翻译是个小技巧，译者往往选择不译，因为它的添加比较随意，并不影响任何的句子结构和句子意义。

②I expect you'll notice that all over the city the cars are left with their wheels being turned towards the side walk so that they can't roll away.

译文：我想你会注意到，全市的汽车在停靠时为了防止滑动，车轮总是向着人行道的。

被动语态不是中文中常用的句型，所以通常译为主动句型，而英文句中则是常见有被动。"expect"的意思比较广泛，口译时要全篇考虑具体的中文选词。

2. 中译英

【原文】

想象这样一个都市环境吧——在那儿，无论是谁，不出半小时，就能置身于美丽的海滩、远足步道以及众多迷人的假日岛屿中。加上阳光明媚的天气、波利尼西亚文化背景，还有美酒佳肴和购物天堂——没错，你脑中的这幅画卷就是新西兰五彩都会奥克兰的真实写照。

除了繁华市景，奥克兰地区还有各式各样的名胜景点和休闲活动，最妙不过的还在于，这些缤纷体验尽在咫尺，来到奥克兰，不同的探险旅程将接踵而至。

美轮美奂的自然乐园

奥克兰多变的地貌景观给游客带去了无限的机会感受自然气息。①西边有茂密的原始雨林，披在山肩，直达壮观的黑沙滩；东边则是轻风低浪的金色沙滩，火红的圣诞树点缀在四周。往北可见连绵起伏的山丘，越过这片葡萄酒产地，就是辽阔海岸；往南，你会发现一片片如诗如画的乡村花园、了无人迹的森林和静谧的水湾。

火山

新西兰的奥克兰地区散落着48座锥形火山，登上任意一个山顶便可饱览城市和海港的壮美风光。许多火山周围都有广阔的绿地，是野餐小憩的完美去处。从奥克兰市中心乘坐渡轮，25分钟便到朗伊托托岛——这是本地最具标志性的火山，也是颇受游客、登山者和观鸟人喜爱的一日游目的地。

豪拉基湾及其群岛

奥克兰的豪拉基湾海洋公园幅员120万公顷，内有绵延海岸、浩瀚海洋和秀美小岛——探索的方式也多种多样。

怀赫科岛堪称豪拉基海湾的冠上明珠，美丽的葡萄园、橄榄林、农地菜畦和金色沙滩组成了这片世外桃源，从奥克兰市中心乘坐渡轮35分钟就能到。在30座精品酒庄中任选一家，品尝屡获殊荣的葡萄佳酿，享受精致美食，欣赏经典的本地艺术。

来到这里就一定要体验水上活动——悠闲的港湾巡游、包船垂钓、观鲸与海豚邂逅之旅，还有海上皮划艇和冲浪，任君挑选。

奥克兰购物与餐饮

奥克兰作为购物狂的天堂，自然少不了从高端设计师精品店到露天集市的奇珍异宝。可到形形色色的咖啡馆和餐厅小坐享用国际美食，也可前往中心城区，感受热力四射的夜生活。温亚德区、维亚达克港、布里托马特区和城市时尚购物区都是人气胜地。

②踏上奥克兰的土地之际，首先要去美景醉人的葡萄酒产区，在葡萄藤绵绵不尽的山丘上，面朝海洋的粼粼波光品尝美酒。

独一无二的城市

新西兰的土著毛利人将此地称作"塔马基马考劳"，意即"拥有倾城之姿的女子"。这里密林遍山，有肥沃的火山土和盛产海鲜的港湾，物产丰富而被各方争抢。至今奥克兰仍保持着全球数一数二的生活品质，不负其经久美誉。

确实，在《美世全球生活质量调查》中奥克兰排名第三，不久前还被《经济学人》选入世界十大宜居城市。

欢迎亲自来体验一下，只要在奥克兰住上几天，参加几个观光行程，一定是开始新西兰之旅的绝佳开始。

【译文】

Imagine an urban environment where everyone lives within half an hour of beautiful beaches, hiking trails and a dozen enchanting holiday islands. Add a sunny climate, a background rhythm of Polynesian culture and a passion for outstanding food, wine and shopping, and you're beginning to get the picture of Auckland, New Zealand, our largest and most diverse city.

More than just a city, Auckland is a whole region full of things to see and do. Best of all, with so many experiences close by it's easy to hop from one adventure to the next.

A stunning natural playground

Auckland's diverse landscapes provide countless opportunities to get immersed in nature. ①In the west, lush native rainforest plunges down the hills to meet the sea on dramatic black sand beaches, while the east's sheltered golden sand beaches are fringed with red-flowering pohutukawa trees. To the north the rolling hills of wine country meet stunning coastlines and in the south you'll find picturesque country gardens, unspoilt forest and tranquil bays to explore.

Volcanoes

New Zealand's Auckland region is dotted with 48 volcanic cones, which provide spectacular panoramic views of the city and harbor. Many are surrounded by lush parkland, making them perfect picnic spots. Rangitoto Island, just a 25-minute ferry ride from downtown Auckland, is the region's most iconic volcano and a favorite day trip destination for visitors, hikers and bird watchers.

Hauraki Gulf and Islands

Auckland's Hauraki Gulf Marine Park encompasses an incredible 1.2 million hectares of coast, sea and islands—and there are so many ways to explore it.

The jewel of the Hauraki Gulf is Waiheke Island, a haven of beautiful vineyards, olive groves, farm land and golden beaches-and only a 35-minute ferry ride away from downtown Auckland. Sip on award-winning wines at some of the 30 boutique vineyards and wineries, enjoy fine dining and pick up superb local artwork.

Make sure you get out on the water while you're here, whether it's a relaxing harbor cruise, a fishing charter, whale and dolphin spotting, diving, kayaking or surfing.

Shopping and dining in Auckland

Auckland is a shopaholic's paradise, with everything from top-end designers to open air street markets. Discover the diverse range of cafes and restaurants offering cuisine from around the globe and check out the buzzing nightlife of the central city.

Favorite spots include Wynyard Quarter, the Viaduct Harbor, the Britomart precinct and City Works Depot.

②Once you've seen the city, head out to one of Auckland's beautiful wine regions where you can sample local wines against the backdrop of vine-covered hills and sparkling ocean.

A city like no other

New Zealand's indigenous Māori people called this land Tāmaki Makaurau, a maiden desired by a hundred lovers. It was a place fought over for its vast riches, including its forested hills, productive volcanic soils and harbors full of seafood. The name still holds true, as Auckland's lifestyle is ranked amongst the best in the world.

In fact, Auckland is rated the third most livable city in the world on the Mercer Quality of Living scale and has just been named as one of the top 10 most livable cities in the world by *The Economist*.

Come and experience it for yourself. A few days in Auckland, building in a tour or two, is the perfect beginning to your New Zealand vacation.

【译文分析】

①西边有茂密的原始雨林,披在山肩,直达壮观的黑沙滩;东边则是轻风低浪的金色沙滩,火红的圣诞树点缀在四周。往北可见连绵起伏的山丘,越过这片葡萄酒产地,就是辽阔海岸;往南,你会发现一片片如诗如画的乡村花园、了无人迹的森林和静谧的水湾。

译文:In the west, lush native rainforest plunges down the hills to meet the sea on dramatic black sand beaches, while the east's sheltered golden sand beaches are fringed with red-flowering pohutukawa trees. To the north the rolling hills of wine country meet stunning coastlines and in the south you'll find picturesque country gardens, unspoilt forest and tranquil bays to explore.

形容词的口译是一个难题,因为中英文对应的意义相差比较大,要能现场译出又要准确表达比较困难,所以尽可能保持大意就可以。但是涉及文化背景的时候还是需要在译前准备中进行充分调研,比如此处的"圣诞树"是新西兰的特别树种"pohutukawa trees"。

②踏上奥克兰的土地之际,首先要去美景醉人的葡萄酒产区,在葡萄藤绵绵不尽的山丘上,面朝海洋的粼粼波光品尝美酒。

译文:Once you've seen the city, head out to one of Auckland's beautiful wine regions where you can sample local wines against the backdrop of vine-covered hills and sparkling ocean.

中文的句式常常有比较多的铺垫,然后出现主句的谓语动词,译者要保持警惕,注意说话人何时结束发言,及时进行调整。在本句当中的地点状语结束之后译者就应该能判断主句的出现。另外,介词的运用也是一个很好的技巧,"against"在此处特别生动。

Ⅴ.技能训练之数字训练

数字一直是口译中的难点,主要是因为中英文中数字存在的方式不同,计量单位有相差,而在日常的口译任务当中,不论是商务话题,还是科技话题都容易出现数字,对译员造成挑战。要解决这个难题就要先认识一下中英文中数字的对应差别,如表 4-1所示。

表 4-1　中英文数字翻译对比

1	一	one
10	十	ten
100	百	1 hundred
1,000	千	1 thousand
10,000	万	10 thousand
100,000	十万	100 thousand
1,000,000	百万	1 million
10,000,000	千万	10 million
100,000,000	亿	100 million
1,000,000,000	十亿	1 billion
10,000,000,000	百亿	10 billion
100,000,000,000	千亿	100 billion
1,000,000,000,000,000	万亿(兆)	1 trillion

在口译过程当中,数字单位的转换对于译员是一个难题,因为单位不同,英文中没有"千、万、千万、亿、百亿、千亿"的单位,而所听到的数字并不会是整数,那么在转换过程中很难把握,所以需要不断地记忆转换练习去掌握正确的数字口译。在口译过程中,对任何的数字都应该做好记录,保持的原则是汉语以四位为一个单位,即"万",而英语以三位为一个单位,即"千",那么这就是常用的"点三杠四法",使用逗号和竖线协助完成记录。

比如,中文数字"八亿七千三百四十五万两千一百九十六",记录为 8|7345|2196,然后加上逗号记录为 8|73,45|2,196 译出来,在英译中则反过来,即"eight hundred seventy three million four hundred fifty two thousand one hundred and ninety six",先记录为 873,452,196,然后加上竖线 8|73,45|2,196,然后再去除逗号,就成了 8|7345|2196。看起来这

个过程很复杂,其实只是对于初学者如此,习惯之后,译员则能很快进行转换。

有的初学译员会单独准备一张记录数字的纸,尤其是在专门练习数字口译时。事先在纸上表明中、英文的各位数字,如下所示(注:b 为 bilbion,m 为 million,th 为 thousand,下同)。

	b			m			th		
	十		千	百	十				
亿,	亿	万	万,	万	万	千,	百	十	个

采用竖式看法,就可以发现单位的对应,标出了中文和英文位数,并有三个分节号。那么在英译中时,就可将数字填在标尺上方,而汉译英时则将数字标在标尺下方,在翻译过程中直接按照目标语标出数字单位译出即可。

比如,eight hundred seventy three million four hundred fifty two thousand one hundred and ninety six,这个数字填入表格则应该是:

	8	7	3,	4	5	2,	1	9	6
	b			m			th		
	十		千	百	十				
亿,	亿	万	万,	万	万	千	百	十	个

读为 eight hundred seventy three million,four hundred fifty two thousand,one hundred and ninety six.

如果是英译中,则记录为:

	b			m			th		
	十		千	百	十				
亿,	亿	万	万,	万	万	千	百	十	个
	8	7	3,	4	5	2,	1	9	6

读为八亿七千三百万四十五万二千一百九十六。

对于数字口译的练习没有尽头,因为有的时候除开数字本身,还会涉及数量单位,而中英文的数量单位有很大差异,还需要译员熟悉转换,如下所示。

1 千米(kilometer)＝0.62 英里(mile)＝2 华里(li)

1 米(meter)＝3.28 英尺(foot)＝1.09 码(yard)

1 千克(kilogram)＝2.20 磅(pound)

1 公升(liter)＝1.76 品脱(pint)＝0.98 加仑(gallon)

还有一些其他的重量单位和距离单位需要熟悉,如果译员不能记住就要及时在现场指出各计量单位之间是需要换算的。

　　有的时候还需要对一些模糊数字进行处理,比如,几个(a few/some/a number of)、十几个(several)、几十个(dozens of)、成百上千(hundreds of)、成千上万(thousands of),等等。

　　数字的口译涵盖广泛,需要译员不断积累经验,勤加练习,冷静处理。

Ⅵ. 词汇拓展

世界遗产委员会 the World Heritage Commission

世界文化遗产保护地 World Heritage Sites（WHS）

中国国家旅游局 China National Tourism Administration

中国国际旅行社 China International Travel Service

旅游管理局 tourist administration bureau

旅行社 travel service/agency

旅游公司 tourism company

环保模范城市 model city for environmental protection

春/秋游 spring/autumn outing

假日旅行 vacation tour

经典路线 classic travel route

目的地 destination

自然景观 natural scenery/attraction

人文景观 places of historic figures and cultural heritage

名山大川 famous mountains and great rivers

名胜古迹 scenic spots and historical sites

佛教名山 famous Buddhist mountain

五岳 China's five great mountains

避暑山庄 mountain resort

度假胜地 holiday resort

避暑胜地 summer resort

自然保护区 nature reserve

国家公园 national park

旅游景点 tourist attraction

古建筑群 ancient architectural complex

园林建筑 garden architecture

山水风光 scenery with mountains and rivers

诱人景色 inviting views

湖光山色 landscape of lakes and hills

青山绿水 green hills and clear waters

景色如画 picturesque views

金石印章 metal and stone seals

石刻碑文 stone inscriptions

天下第一泉 the finest spring under heaven

石舫 stone boat

水榭 waterside house

莲花池 lotus pond

国画 traditional Chinese painting

山水/水墨画 landscape/ink painting

手工艺品 artifact/handicrafts

陶器 earthenware

折扇 folding fan

木/竹/贝雕 wood/bamboo/shell carving

休闲旅游 packaged leisure travel

江南水乡 south of the lower reaches of the Yangtze River

历史文化名村名镇 towns and villages with rich historical and cultural heritage

美丽宜居乡村 a countryside that is beautiful and pleasant to live in

领略自然景观的魅力 appreciate the charms of natural landscape

四面环海 be surrounded by sea

国家级重点风景名胜区 state-level scenic spot

世界七大奇迹 seven wonders of the world

巴比伦空中花园 the Hanging Gardens of Babylon

阿尔忒弥斯神庙 the Temple of Artemis（Diana）at Ephesus

宙斯神像 the Statue of Zeus

摩索拉斯陵墓 the Mausoleum at Halicarnassus

罗德岛太阳神巨像 the Colossus of Rhodes

亚历山大灯塔 the Pharos（Lighthouse）of Alexandria

埃及金字塔 the Pyramids of Egypt

人与自然和谐共生 harmony between humankind and nature

美丽中国建设 Beautiful China Initiative

资源节约型、环境友好型社会 resource-conserving，environmentally friendly society

国家生态文明试区 national ecological conservation pilot zone

重点生态功能区 important ecological area（IEA）

绿色低碳循环发展产业体系 industrial system geared toward green，low-carbon，and circular development

绿色金融 green finance

循环发展引领计划 initiative to guide the shift toward circular development

近零碳排放区示范工程 initiative to demonstrate near-zero carbon emissions zones

生态安全屏障 eco-security shield

江河源头和水源涵养区生态保护 ecological protection of river sources and water source conservative areas

蓝色海湾整治行动 Blue Bay Initiative

农村人居环境整治行动 rural living environment improvement initiative

节约优先、保护优先、自然恢复为主。

Give priority to conserving resources，protecting the environment，and letting nature restore itself.

绿水青山就是金山银山。

Lucid waters and lush mountains are invaluable assets.

桂林山水甲天下，阳朔山水甲桂林。

Guilin landscape tops those elsewhere，and Yangshuo landscape tops that of Guilin.

上有天堂下有苏杭。

As there is the paradise in heaven，so there are Suzhou and Hangzhou on earth.

五岳归来不看山，黄山归来不看岳。

Trips to China's five great mountains render trips to other mountain unnecessary，and a trip to Huangshan renders trips to the five great mountains unnecessary.

黄山四绝 the four unique scenic features：picturesque rocks，legendary pines，the sea of clouds and hot springs

参考文献

[1] 王学文. 口译实训[M]. 北京：外文出版社,2015.

[2] 吴冰. 现代汉译英口译教程[M]. 北京：外语教学与研究出版社,2011.

[3] http：//www.newzealand.com.

[4] http：//www.youth.cn/.

第五章 文化交流

Ⅰ. 词汇预习

incarnation 化身

needle therapy 针灸疗法

terracotta warriors 兵马俑

legion 军团

UNESCO 联合国教科文组织

World Cultural Heritage 世界文化遗产

World Intangible Cultural Heritage 世界非物质文化遗产

mythology 神话

perfunctory 敷衍的

vicissitudes 变迁

nourishment 营养

envoy 使节

alfalfa 苜蓿

pomegranate 石榴

flax 胡麻

sesame 芝麻

colored glaze 彩釉

bustle 繁忙

magnitude 巨大

friction 冲突

bewilderment 疑惑

dominant 占优势的

digestion 消化

integration 融合

innovation 创新

indigenous 本土的

Confucianism 儒家文化

Taoism 道教文化

etiquette 礼仪

pilgrimage 朝圣

Buddhist scriptures 佛经

fortitude 坚韧

movable-type printing 活字印刷术

Renaissance 文艺复兴

porcelain 瓷器

Coventry Cathedral 考文垂大教堂

reconciliation 和解

truce 休战

Crumlin Road Gaol 克拉姆林路监狱

referendum 公投

Ebola 埃博拉（病毒）

Ⅱ. 典型句型

1. 中译英

（1）万里长城雄伟壮观。古代中国人在没有机械的条件下用双手修建了这样伟大的建筑真是了不起。

The Great Wall is magnificent. It is really great that the ancient Chinese constructed such a gigantic structure without any machinery available.

（2）回到宋代，大约 11 世纪，人们开始玩一个叫蹴鞠的游戏，这被看作是足球古老的起源。

Back to the Song Dynasty，about the 11th century，people started to play a game called Cuju，which is regarded as the origin of ancient football.

（3）书法是中国文化的精髓。书法在中国随处可见，与日常生活紧密相连。

Calligraphy is the essence of Chinese culture. It can be found everywhere in China，and is closely linked to daily life.

（4）在中国的传统文化中，剪纸可以反映生活的许多方面，如繁荣、健康或收获。

In traditional Chinese culture，paper-cuts can reflect various aspects of life such as prosperity，health or harvest.

（5）太极拳基于以柔克刚的原理，发端于中国古代，最开始是一种武术和自卫方式。

Taijiquan is based on the principle of the soft overcoming the hard and originated in ancient China as a martial art and a means of self-defense.

2. 英译中

（1）Along with King Tut，perhaps no figure is more famously associated with ancient Egypt than Cleopatra Ⅶ.

说到古埃及，人们能想到的著名人物除图特王外，恐怕就剩埃及艳后克娄巴特拉七世了。

（2）At traditional Filipino wedding receptions，the bride and groom release two doves into the air to represent a long，peaceful，and harmonious life together.

在菲律宾举行婚礼时，新娘和新郎会放飞两只鸽子，一只代表长久平安，一只代表幸福美满的生活。

（3）The ancient Chinese needle therapy has been around in the UK for many years.

中国古老的针灸疗法在英国已经有很多年的历史了。

（4）In many countries of the world，the celebration of Christmas on December 25th is a high point of the year.

在世界上的许多国家，12 月 25 日的圣诞节庆是全年的一个亮点。

（5）Thanksgiving is a day for food and football，and for hoping the turkey didn't turn out too dry.

感恩节是分享美食、观赏球赛的日子，大家都希望火鸡不要烤得太干。

Ⅲ. 段落翻译

1. 中译英

【原文】

大家都知道，中国有秦俑，人们称之为"地下的军团"。法国总统希拉克参观之后说："不看金字塔，不算真正到过埃及。不看秦俑，不算真正到过中国。"1987 年，这一尘封了2000 多年的中华文化珍品被列入世界文化遗产。中国还有大量文明成果被教科文组织列入世界文化遗产、世界非物质文化遗产和世界记忆遗产名录。

【译文】

I assume you have all heard of China's terracotta warriors, the buried legions of Emperor Qin. After his visit to the site, President Chirac of France said that a visit to

Egypt will not be complete without seeing the pyramids，and that a visit to China will not be complete without seeing the terracotta warriors. In 1987，this national treasure of China，buried underground for over two thousand years，was put on the UNESCO World Cultural Heritage list. There are many more proud Chinese achievements that have been included in the World Cultural Heritage list，the World Intangible Cultural Heritage list and the Memory of the World list.

2. 英译中

【原文】

American mythology loves nothing more than the reluctant hero：the man—it is usually a man—whose natural talents have destined him for more than obliging obscurity. George Washington，we are told，was a leader who would have preferred to have been a farmer. Thomas Jefferson，a writer. Martin Luther King，Jr.，a preacher. These men were roused from lives of perfunctory achievement，our legends have it，not because they chose their own exceptionalism，but because we，the people，chose it for them. We—seeing greatness in them that they were too humble to observe themselves—conferred on them uncommon paths. Historical circumstance became its own call of duty，and the logic of democracy proved itself through the answer.

【译文】

在美式神话中，主角通常是那些不知不觉中成为的英雄：一般而言，他就是一个人，因禀赋异常，注定此生不能默默无闻。乔治·华盛顿原本更愿意当农民，而不是领导国家；托马斯·杰弗逊，曾立志要成为一名作家；而马丁·路德·金只是一名牧师。据说是公众要求他们不能敷衍塞责，埋没才华；是我们要求这些伟人必须振作起来，追求卓越。我们选择了他们，是因为我们看到他们的伟大——尽管他们谦虚地认为自己并不出众——是我们把他们推上了不寻常的人生道路。换言之，历史境遇和民主体制造就了这些英雄。

Ⅳ. 篇章翻译

1. 中文原文

中华文明经历了5000多年的历史变迁，但始终一脉相承，积淀着中华民族最深层的精神追求，代表着中华民族独特的精神标识，为中华民族生生不息、发展壮大提供了丰厚滋养。①中华文明是在中国大地上产生的文明，也是同其他文明不断交流互鉴而形成的文明。

公元前100多年，中国就开始开辟通往西域的丝绸之路。②汉代张骞于公元前138

年和 119 年两次出使西域,向西域传播了中华文化,也引进了葡萄、苜蓿、石榴、胡麻、芝麻等西域作物。西汉时期,中国的船队就到达了印度和斯里兰卡,用中国的丝绸换取了琉璃、珍珠等物品。中国唐代是中国历史上对外交流的活跃期。据史料记载,唐代中国通使交好的国家达 70 多个,那时候的首都长安里来自各国的使臣、商人、留学生云集成群。这个大交流促进了中华文化远播世界,也促进了各国文化和物产传入中国。15 世纪初,中国明代著名航海家郑和七次远洋航海,到了东南亚很多国家,一直抵达非洲东海岸的肯尼亚,留下了中国同沿途各国人民友好交往的佳话。明末清初,中国人积极学习现代科技知识,欧洲的天文学、医学、数学、几何学、地理学知识纷纷传入中国,开阔了中国人的知识视野。之后,中外文明交流互鉴更是频繁展开,这其中有冲突、矛盾、疑惑、拒绝,但更多是学习、消化、融合、创新。

佛教产生于古代印度,但传入中国后,经过长期演化,佛教同中国儒家文化和道家文化融合发展,最终形成了具有中国特色的佛教文化,给中国人的宗教信仰、哲学观念、文学艺术、礼仪习俗等留下了深刻影响。中国唐代玄奘西行取经,历尽磨难,体现的是中国人学习域外文化的坚韧精神。根据他的故事演绎的神话小说《西游记》,我想大家都知道。中国人根据中华文化发展了佛教思想,形成了独特的佛教理论,而且使佛教从中国传播到了日本、韩国、东南亚等地。

2000 多年来,佛教、伊斯兰教、基督教等先后传入中国,中国音乐、绘画、文学等也不断吸纳外来文明的优长。中国传统画法同西方油画融合创新,形成了独具魅力的中国写意油画,徐悲鸿等大师的作品受到广泛赞赏。中国的造纸术、火药、印刷术、指南针四大发明带动了世界变革,推动了欧洲文艺复兴。中国哲学、文学、医药、丝绸、瓷器、茶叶等传入西方,渗入西方民众日常生活之中。《马可·波罗游记》令无数人对中国心向往之。

【译文】

Having gone through over 5,000 years of vicissitudes, the Chinese civilization has always kept to its original root. As the unique cultural identity of the Chinese nation, it contains our most profound cultural pursuits and provides us with abundant nourishment for existence and development. ①The Chinese civilization, though born on the soil of China, has come to its present form through constant exchanges and mutual learning with other civilizations.

In the 2nd century B.C., China began working on the Silk Road leading to the Western Regions. ②In 138 B.C. and 119 B.C., Envoy Zhang Qian of the Han Dynasty made two trips to those regions, spreading the Chinese culture there and bringing into China grape, alfalfa, pomegranate, flax, sesame and other products. In the Western Han Dynasty, China's merchant fleets sailed as far as India and Sri Lanka where they traded China's silk for colored glaze, pearls and other products. The Tang Dynasty saw dynamic interactions between China and other countries. According to historical documents, the dynasty exchanged envoys with over 70 countries, and Chang'an, the capital of Tang, bustled with envoys, merchants and students from other countries. Exchanges of such a magnitude helped the spread of the Chinese culture to the rest of the world and the introduction into China of the cultures and products from other countries. In the early 15th century, Zheng He, the famous navigator of China's Ming Dynasty, made seven expeditions to the Western Seas, reaching many Southeast Asian countries and even Kenya on the east coast of Africa. These trips left behind many good stories of friendly exchanges between the people of China and countries along the route. In late Ming Dynasty and early Qing Dynasty, the Chinese people began to learn modern science and technology with great zeal, as the European knowledge of astronomy, medicine, mathematics, geometry and geography were being introduced into China, which helped broaden the horizon of the Chinese people. Thereafter, exchanges and mutual learning between the Chinese civilization and other civilizations became more frequent. There were indeed conflicts, frictions, bewilderment and denial in this process. But the more dominant features of the period were learning, digestion, integration and innovation.

Buddhism originated in ancient India. After it was introduced into China, the religion went through an extended period of integrated development with the indigenous Confucianism and Taoism and finally became the Buddhism with Chinese characteristics, thus making a deep impact on the religious belief, philosophy, literature, art, etiquette and customs of the Chinese people. Xuanzang (Hiuen Tsang), the Tang monk who endured untold sufferings as he went on a pilgrimage to the west for Buddhist scriptures, gave full expression to the determination and fortitude of the Chinese people to learn from other cultures. I am sure that you have all heard about the Chinese classics *Journey to the West*, which was written on the basis of his stories. The Chinese people have enriched Buddhism in the light of Chinese culture and developed some special Buddhist thoughts. Moreover, they also helped Buddhism spread from China to Japan, Republic of Korea, Southeast Asia and beyond.

In the course of some two thousand years and more, Buddhism, Islam and Christianity have been introduced into China successively, which allowed the country's music, painting and literature to benefit from the advantages of other civilizations. China's freehand oil painting is an innovative combination of China's traditional painting and the Western oil painting, and the works of Xu Beihong and other masters have been widely acclaimed. China's Four Great Inventions, namely, papermaking, gunpowder, movable-type printing and compass, led to great changes in the world, including the European Renaissance. China's philosophy, literature, medicine, silk, porcelain and tea reached the West and became part of people's daily life. *The Travels of Marco Polo* generated a widespread interest in China.

【译文分析】

①中华文明是在中国大地上产生的文明,也是同其他文明不断交流互鉴而形成的文明。

译文：The Chinese civilization, though born on the soil of China, has come to its present form through constant exchanges and mutual learning with other civilizations.

中文属于意和文字,英文属于形和文字,在此句中文中的关系看上去像是并列关系,实际上更加强调中华文明与其他文明的交流互鉴,所以在翻译成英文的时候,可以适当加上表示逻辑转折关系的连词"though"使意思表达更清晰。

②汉代张骞于公元前138年和119年两次出使西域。

译文：In 138 B.C. and 119 B.C., Envoy Zhang Qian of the Han Dynasty made two trips to those regions.

在此句中因为中国人都知道张骞是汉代的使节,所以在中文中没有特别点明他的身份,但在介绍给西方人时,可能西方人并不一定知道张骞的身份,所以在翻译的时候需要加上"Envoy"一词来补充介绍其身份。在翻译下文中的"唐代玄奘"时同样需要补上"Monk"一词"Xuanzang, the Tang Monk"。

2. 英译中

【原文】

In the ruins of the old Coventry Cathedral is a sculpture of a man and a woman reaching out to embrace each other. ①The sculptor was inspired by the story of a woman who crossed Europe on foot after the war to find her husband.

Casts of the same sculpture can be found in Belfast and Berlin, and it is simply called Reconciliation.

②Reconciliation is the peaceful end to conflict, and we were reminded of this in August when countries on both sides of the First World War came together to remember in peace.

The ceramic poppies at the Tower of London drew millions, and the only possible reaction to seeing them and walking among them was silence. For every poppy a life; and a reminder of the grief of loved ones left behind.

No one who fought in that war is still alive, but we remember their sacrifice and indeed the sacrifice of all those in the armed forces who serve and protect us today.

In 1914, many people thought the war would be over by Christmas, but sadly by then the trenches were dug and the future shape of the war in Europe was set.

But, as we know, something remarkable did happen that Christmas, exactly a hundred years ago today.

Without any instruction or command, the shooting stopped and German and British soldiers met in No Man's Land. Photographs were taken and gifts exchanged. It was a Christmas truce.

Truces are not a new idea. In the ancient world a truce was declared for the duration of the Olympic Games and wars and battles were put on hold.

Sport has a wonderful way of bringing together people and nations, as we saw this year in Glasgow when over 70 countries took part in the Commonwealth Games.

It is no accident that they are known as the Friendly Games. As well as promoting dialogue between nations, the Commonwealth Games pioneered the inclusion of para-sports within each day's events.

As with the Invictus Games that followed, the courage, determination and talent of the athletes captured our imagination as well as breaking down divisions.

The benefits of reconciliation were clear to see when I visited Belfast in June. While my tour of the set of *Game of Thrones* may have gained most attention, my visit to the Crumlin Road Gaol will remain vividly in my mind.

What was once a prison during the Troubles is now a place of hope and fresh purpose; a reminder of what is possible when people reach out to one another, rather like the couple in the sculpture.

Of course, reconciliation takes different forms. In Scotland after the referendum many felt great disappointment, while others felt great relief; and bridging these differences will take time.

Bringing reconciliation to war or emergency zones is an even harder task, and I have been deeply touched this year by the selflessness of aid workers and medical volunteers who have gone abroad to help victims of conflict or of diseases like Ebola, often at great personal risk.

For me, the life of Jesus Christ, the Prince of Peace, whose birth we celebrate today, is an inspiration and an anchor in my life.

A role model of reconciliation and forgiveness, he stretched out his hands in love, acceptance and healing. Christ's example has taught me to seek to respect and value all people, of whatever faith or none.

Sometimes it seems that reconciliation stands little chance in the face of war and discord. But, as the Christmas truce a century ago reminds us, peace and goodwill have lasting power in the hearts of men and women.

On that chilly Christmas Eve in 1914, many of the German forces sang *Silent Night*, its haunting melody inching across the line.

That carol is still much-loved today, a legacy of the Christmas truce, and a reminder to us all that even in the unlikeliest of places hope can still be found.

【译文】

在旧考文垂大教堂废墟的外面竖立着一尊雕塑,造型是一个男人和一个女人伸着手想要拥抱彼此。①雕塑的灵感来源于一个女人在战争爆发后徒步跨越欧洲寻找自己丈夫的故事。

在贝尔法斯特和柏林都能找到同样的雕塑,它的名字很简单,叫做和解。

②和解是战争过后的和平,今年 8 月第一次世界大战的交战双方在一起纪念和平时,我们再次想到了"和解"这个词。

伦敦塔的陶瓷罂粟吸引了数百万人,人们看到这场景并从中穿过时的唯一反应是沉默。每一朵罂粟象征着一个生命,让人们想起失去至爱后的悲痛。

也不能忘记那些依然在服务和保卫着我们的军中将士做出的奉献。

1914 年,很多人认为战争会在圣诞节结束,但遗憾的是那时战壕已经挖好,欧洲战场上未来的战争形态也已经确定。

不过,正如我们知道的那样,一百年前的今天,也就是圣诞节当天,的确发生了一件意义非凡的事情。

没有指示,没有命令,射击停止了,德国士兵和英国士兵相聚在无人地带。士兵们拍照留念并互赠礼物。这就是圣诞节休战协定。

休战协定并非新创。古时候战争和战斗都要在奥运会期间暂停。

运动是将人们和国家聚在一起的好方法,我们看到有 70 多个国家参与今年在格拉斯哥举行的英联邦运动会。

这个运动会被称为友好运动会并非偶然。除了促进国家之间的对话以外,英联邦运动会还开创了在每天的比赛项目中都加入残疾运动项目的先河。

在之后的不可征服运动会中,运动员们的勇气,决心和天赋不但吸引着我们的目光,同时还打破了隔阂。

今年六月份我访问贝尔法斯特时就清楚地看到了和解的好处。虽然我参观《权力的游戏》拍摄地的新闻吸引了大部分人的注意力,但对克拉姆林路监狱的参观却让我记忆犹新。

这个在北爱尔兰动乱期间的监狱如今充满了希望和新目标；让人们认识到，当人们伸出手互相帮助时，什么事都是有可能的，就像雕塑里的那对夫妇一样。

当然，和解有很多方式。苏格兰公投后，很多人觉得很失望，有的人却觉得很宽慰，弥合这些分歧尚需时日。

在战争中或者紧急突发地带取得和解更是困难，今年，救援人员和医疗志愿者们不顾个人安危，奔赴国外帮助冲突地区的受害人员或者饱受疾病（例如埃博拉）困扰的病人。我深为所动。

今天是耶稣基督，和平之主的诞辰，庆祝他的生日对我来说是一种鼓舞，是我生命中的一个精神支柱。

作为和解和宽恕的榜样，他伸出充满爱、接纳和弥合的手。耶稣教会我尊重和珍视每一个人，无关信仰。

有时候和解在战争与冲突面前似乎无力反击。但，正如一百年前的圣诞节停战协定，和平和美好的希望在世人心里拥有持久的影响力。

1914 年的圣诞节前夜很寒冷，德国士兵们吟唱的《平安夜》穿过交火线，让人难以忘怀。

今天，这首圣诞歌曲依然受欢迎，它是圣诞节停战协定的延续，也提醒着我们，即使在最不可能的地方，依然可以找到希望。

【译文分析】

①The sculptor was inspired by the story of a woman who crossed Europe on foot after the war to find her husband.

译文：雕塑的灵感来源于一个女人在战争爆发后徒步跨越欧洲寻找自己丈夫的故事。

在此句的翻译中，可进行词性的转换，原来的谓语动词"赋……以灵感"改为名词"灵感"，"sculptor"（雕塑）在原句中充当主语，翻译过来充当定语。

②Reconciliation is the peaceful end to conflict, and we were reminded of this in August when countries on both sides of the First World War came together to remember in peace.

译文：和解是战争过后的和平，今年 8 月第一次世界大战的交战双方在一起纪念和平时，我们再次想到了"和解"这个词。

英语中的时间状语往往放在句子的后面，翻译成中文时要注意调整语序。在口译时要注意完整地听到一个概念再做决定语序调整，但是如果有把握对句式的理解是正确的，为了对时间进行很好的同步，也允许对句式进行适当的调整。

Ⅴ. 技能训练之表达能力训练

　　口译译员要具备好的表达能力,不仅要做到发音准确、语调适宜,还应准确、清晰、连贯、得体地向听众传达发言者的立场和观点。译员需要在理解的基础上对语言进行逻辑分析与整合,在口译过程中监控自己的口译表达。口译的基本要求是"形变"而"意存","形转"而"意达";口译的职业标准是"意及"而又"神似","意传"而又"讯达"。

　　口译译员尤其需要提高语用能力。鲍晓英、钱明丹认为口译员的语用能力主要表现为"是否能准确理解话语中含有交际文化的词语、习惯表达方式、礼貌套语、称呼语等社会文化语言表达法,并在译文中适当调整,进行自然得体的表达"。学生译员只有了解不同社会的交际文化差异,对语言变体、语域、文化所指与修辞语等有较强的敏感力,才能在口译时减少语用的失误。

　　口译表达能力的提高需要"灵活使用普通的小词、常见词、概括性强的词来释义或意译,区分同义词、近义词,以及词的搭配等"。平时积累过程中应多注意对词的语境进行分析。口译时用词要严谨,还要注意语气的表达。

　　口译译员一方面要能听懂不同国籍的人所讲的英语,并熟悉我国的一些方言;另一方面,译员口译时自己不能带有方言,要做到发音准确。学生译员可以将自己的口译录音,通过交换听,从而互相修正对方发音方面的错误。

　　此外,扩大知识面有助于表达能力的提高。增加百科知识,包括对政策的了解、跟踪国内外形势的发展等。就商务知识而言,还应增加与管理、贸易、营销、金融和法律等相关的知识。口译若是涉及专业交流方面,译员需要熟悉特定的词汇和表达法;若是涉及外交或对外谈判方面,译员一定要熟记固定政策的译法,不但用词和表达法不能错,时态也不能错。

　　口译表达技能的训练可以根据口译的形式与内容的差异而有针对性地进行。外交口译通常要求译者"要始终保持声音洪亮,并善于在不同场合调整对声音的控制,语音要准确、清晰、表达要有韵律,要流畅,使听众感到易懂舒适"。一场好的口译应该"神形兼顾,达意传神,声情并茂",因此译员需要进行公共演讲训练。

口译训练

1. 中译英

【原文】

　　"未之见而亲焉,可以往矣;久而不忘焉,可以来矣。"来到阿拉伯国家,我和我的同事们都有一种亲近感。这是因为,在穿越时空的往来中,中阿两个民族彼此真诚相待,在古丝绸之路上出入相友,在争取民族独立的斗争中甘苦与共,在建设国家的征程上守望相助。这份信任牢不可破,是金钱买不到的。

【译文】

An ancient Chinese philosopher said，"Visit those who you feel close to even without meeting them before，and invite those you cannot forget long after your paths crossed." Coming to the Arab world，my colleagues and I all feel a sense of affinity. This is because in their exchanges across time and space，the Chinese and Arab peoples have been sincere with each other，forging friendship along the ancient Silk Road，sharing weal and woe in the fight for national independence，and helping each other in building their own countries. Such trust is unbreakable and cannot be bought with money.

2. 英译中

【原文】

We want to see Chinese youngsters here，American youngsters in China，and we want to see them breaking down the barriers that exist between any peoples from different cultures and experiences and histories and backgrounds. And I think that will happen because in ways that were unimaginable just a few years ago，young people in both China and the United States are global citizens. They are communicating with new tools of technology that were not even dreamt of a decade ago. And so they are already building cyber or Internet relationships，and we want to give them a chance to form the real deal—getting to know each other，getting to understand each other.

【译文】

我们希望在这里看到中国的年轻人,而在中国能看到美国的年轻人,我们希望他们能够打破任何存在于不同文化、经历、历史、背景的人之间的障碍。我认为这会实现,因为中美两国的年轻人已经以仅在短短几年前还不可想象的方式变成全球公民。他们在用十年前想都想不到的新技术工具进行交流。因此他们已经在建立网际或因特网关系了,而我们希望给他们一个机会去形成一种货真价实的关系——相互认识,相互理解。

Ⅵ. 词汇拓展

文化多样性 cultural diversity

文化交流 cultural exchange

本土文化 native culture

刺绣 embroidery

书法 calligraphy

孟子 Mencius

战国 Warring States

《诗经》*The Book of Songs*

《水浒》*Water Margin / Outlaws of the Marsh*

《本草纲目》*Compendium of Materia Medical*

除夕 Chinese New Year's Eve/Eve of the Spring Festival

对联（Spring Festival）Couplets

农历 lunar calendar

叩头 kowtow

泼水节 Water-Splashing Day

腊八节 the Laba Rice Porridge Festival

门当户对 perfect Match/exact Match

文房四宝（笔墨纸砚）The Four Treasure of the Study（Brush，Inkstick，Paper，and Inkstone）

甲骨文 Oracle Bone Inscriptions

敦煌莫高窟 Mogao Caves

夫子庙 The Confucian Temple

亭/阁 pavilion/attic

追星族 star struck

相声 cross-talk/comic Dialogue

电视小品 TV sketch/TV skit

古装片 costume drama

木偶戏 puppet show

谜语 riddle

烟花爆竹 fireworks and firecracker

天干地支 the heavenly stems and earthly branches

图腾 totem

十四行诗 sonnet

诺亚方舟 Noah's Ark

滑铁卢 Waterloo

缪斯 Muse

潘多拉的盒子 Pandora's Box

斯芬克司之谜 Riddle of the Sphinx

象牙塔 Ivory Tower

硅谷 Silicon Valley

多米诺骨牌 Dominoes

参考文献

[1] 鲍晓英，钱明丹.学生口译语用能力培养模式构建[J].外语界，2013(1)：88-94.

[2] 何群，李春怡.外交口译[M].北京：外语教学与研究出版社，2011.

[3] 吴冰.关于口译教材编写的思考——兼评国内出版的六种教材[J].外语教学与研究，1999(2)：49-54.

[4] 杨玮斌.论口译实践的三个要素[J].上海翻译，2012(2)：51-55.

[5] http：//www.fmprc.gov.cn/mfa_eng.

[6] http：//www.kekenet.com/kouyi/.

[7] http：//www.yeeworld.com.

第六章　商务谈判

Ⅰ. 词汇预习

quotation 报价

claim 索赔

price adjustment 调价

counter-offer 还盘

price-versus-performance ratio 性价比

consumer group 消费群

the letter of guarantee 担保函

rock bottom price 最低价

infrastructure 基础建设

private financing 私有融资

cost effectively 节约成本

long-term trade relations 长期业务关系

coincide with 与……一致

credit standing 信用

chamber of commerce 商会

Jeen Thai Phee Nong Gan 中泰一家亲

setting up an RMB clearing bank 设立人民币清算银行

connectivity 互联互通

Sanpower Group 三胞集团

Fraser Group 弗雷泽集团

NVC Lighting 雷士照明公司

Dynex 丹尼克斯

Covpress 英国考普莱公司

supply chain 供应链

Pinsent Masons 品诚梅森律师事务所

China-Britain Business Council（CBBC）英中贸易协会

UK Trade and Investment(UKTI)英国贸易投资署

Ⅱ．典型句型

1. 中译英

【原文】

(1) 公司的财务负担不了。

It is beyond the company's financial capacity.

(2) 此事如再发生，你方将招致索赔。

If this happens again，you will be liable to claim.

(3) 我方将投保这种险别，费用由你方承担。

We shall provide such insurance at your cost.

(4) 我方的报价是优惠的，我们的调价是有限的，目前我们无法接受您的还盘。

Our quotation is favorable in your interest，and there is a limit to our price adjustment. Currently we just cannot accept your counter-offer.

(5) 我们的新产品有着最好的性价比，所以有比较稳定的消费群。

Our products enjoy the best price-versus-performance ratio and therefore have a stable consumer group.

2. 英译中

【原文】

(1) The letter of guarantee should reach us two months before shipment is due，as stipulated in contract.

担保函必须在合同规定的装运期前两个月到达我方。

(2) I'm afraid we can't reduce the price of this brand of shirt. You know，$20.15 is our rock bottom price. If you purchase more than 10,000 units，we can reduce it to $19.

恐怕我们不能降低这个品牌衬衣的价格。20.15 美元已经是我们的最低价了。如果你能买 1 万件以上的话，我们可以把单价降到 19 美元。

(3) This makes UK your natural partner because our record on innovation and discovery is envied across the world.

这说明了英国能成为你们的自然合作伙伴，因为我们在革新与探索方面所取得的成就令世界羡慕不已。

(4) We are a leader in the development of public-private partnerships，which involve

the public and the private sector working together to provide infrastructure and services.

我们在公共与私有合作方面处于世界领先水平，也就是公共部门和私有部门之间进行合作从事基础建设和提供服务。

（5）The private financing initiatives have enabled us to develop our infrastructure more cost effectively，more quickly and to a higher quality.

私有融资的启动让我们能够在基础建设方面成本更节约、速度更快、质量更高。

Ⅲ. 对话翻译

A：Mr. Chen，another purpose of my coming here is to inquire about possibilities of establishing long-term trade relations with your company.

A：陈先生，我此行另一个目的是想探询与贵公司建立长期业务关系的可能性。

B：Your desire to establish long-term business relations with us coincides with ours，but I don't know much about your company.

B：你方想与我方建立长期业务关系的愿望与我方是一致的，但是我对贵公司并不是很了解。

A：Concerning our financial position，credit standing and trade reputation，you may refer to New York Branch，the Bank of China，or to our local chamber of commerce.

A：关于我们的财务状况、信用、声誉，可向中国银行纽约分行或当地商会进行了解。

B：Thank you for your information. I think that establishing business relations between us will be beneficial to both of us.

B：感谢你方提供的信息。我想我们之间建立业务关系，将有益于我们双方。

A：This is my first visit to your company. I'd appreciate your kind consideration in the coming negotiations.

A：这是我初次拜访贵公司，在日后的洽谈中请你多加关照。

B：We are very happy to be of help. I can assure you of our close cooperation.

B：我们十分乐意协助，并且保证全力合作。

Ⅳ. 篇章翻译

1. 中译英

【原文】

当前，国际形势继续发生深刻复杂变化，亚洲正成为世界经济最具活力和潜力的地区,东亚的地位和作用日益上升。中泰面临深化合作的良好机遇。我们是老朋友,也是好亲戚。①在新形势下,应巩固"中泰一家亲"的传统情谊,谱写"亲上加亲"的友好新篇章,也就是成为以诚相待的好朋友,密切合作的好伙伴,频繁往来的好亲戚。让中泰友好之花结出更加丰硕的果实,推动两国全面战略合作伙伴关系迈上新台阶。相信议员们一定会为中泰友好投赞成票。在此,我愿提出以下建议:

第一,共谋未来发展。中泰高层交流频繁的传统应当继续发扬。中方欢迎贵国领导人多到中国参观访问,中方也将安排高级别代表团经常访泰。双方合作既要立足当前,落实好已商定的项目,更要着眼长远,从战略上统筹规划。此访期间,双方将共同发表"关于中泰关系发展远景规划的联合新闻公报",为未来合作指明方向。中方愿结合泰国国家发展战略规划,与泰方一起推进交通、水利、能源、教育等各领域合作。

第二,深化务实合作。经贸合作是两国友好关系的重要支撑。中方愿与泰方一道落实好两国战略性合作共同行动计划,推动各领域互利合作。力争提前实现2015年双边贸易额1000亿美元目标。②泰国盛产大米等农产品,中方充分考虑这一情况,愿支持本国企业在今后5年内进口100万吨泰国大米,并将根据实际需求考虑扩大规模。橡胶是中泰贸易的重要商品,中方愿积极考虑从泰国增加进口橡胶。我们还将建立专门的机制,探讨农产品贸易合作。随着两国公民频繁来往和经济联系日益密切,中方愿积极考虑在泰设立人民币清算银行,鼓励两国企业更多使用本币进行双边贸易结算。

第三,加快互联互通。交通等基础设施不仅是经济社会发展的基础,也是增进睦邻友好的纽带。铁路合作可以成为中泰合作的新亮点。中国拥有先进的高铁建设能力和丰富的管理经验,泰国推进铁路等基础设施建设有利于物流畅通、经济繁荣。两国加强铁路建设合作潜力巨大,中方对此持积极态度。我此行将与英拉总理共同出席"中国高铁展",希望双方早日启动实质性合作。中方还将同泰方一起,积极开展电力、电网、可再生能源等方面合作,共同实施好水利建设项目。

【译文】

Now that the international situation continues to undergo profound and complex changes,Asia has stood out as the most vibrant and promising region in the global economy,and the status and role of East Asia have been on the increase. China and Thailand are presented with golden opportunities to deepen cooperation. We are old friends and close relatives. ①Under the new circumstances,we need to cement the traditional ties of "Jeen Thai Phee Nong Gan" and write a new chapter of even closer friendship. Our two countries are determined to become good friends that treat each other sincerely, good partners engaged in close cooperation and good relatives that visit each other frequently, so that the blossoming flower of China-Thailand friendship will yield more fruits and the comprehensive strategic cooperative partnership will reach a new height. I am sure that the honorable members of the National Assembly will vote yes for this friendship. In this connection, I would like to suggest the following:

First, we need to jointly plan for future development. The fine tradition of regular high-level engagement should be carried forward. China welcomes more visits by leaders of Thailand. China, on its part, will also send high-level delegations to Thailand on a frequent basis. We should base our cooperation on real needs and earnestly implement the mutually-agreed projects. More importantly, we should take a long-term and strategic perspective and make overall plans. During my visit, the two sides will release a joint press communique on the Long-term Program on the Development of China-Thailand Relations, charting the course for future cooperation. China is ready to work with Thailand to boost cooperation in wide-ranging areas including transport, water conservancy, energy and education in light of Thailand's strategic plan for national development.

Second, we need to deepen practical cooperation. Economic and trade cooperation is an important anchor for our friendly ties. China will work with Thailand to implement the Joint Action Plan on Chinese-Thai Strategic Cooperation to advance mutually beneficial cooperation across the board. The two sides need to strive to reach, ahead of schedule, the goal of US $ 100 billion in two-way trade set for 2015. ② Thailand is a main producer of rice and other agricultural products. China is well aware of this and will support Chinese companies in importing one million tons of rice from Thailand in the next five years and consider increasing that amount further in light of actual demand. Rubber is an important commodity in our trade. China will actively consider importing more rubber from Thailand. We will also establish a specialized mechanism to explore trade cooperation on agricultural products. As our personnel and economic exchanges get closer, China will actively consider setting up an RMB clearing bank in Thailand and hopes that Chinese and Thai companies will settle more cross-border trade in our respective currencies.

Third, we need to speed up connectivity development. Infrastructure such as transportation facilities forms not only the basis for economic and social development, but also a bond of good-neighborliness and friendship. Railway cooperation can become a new highlight in China-Thailand cooperation. China has leading capacity in high-speed rail construction and rich managerial expertise. Railway development in Thailand will facilitate smooth logistics and economic prosperity. There is enormous potential for railway cooperation between our two countries and China is keen to advance such cooperation. During my visit，Prime Minister Yingluck and I will together attend the China high-speed rail exhibition. I hope to see early launch of substantive cooperation between the two sides. China and Thailand will also carry out vigorous cooperation in electricity，power grid and renewable energy and work together to ensure the sound implementation of water projects.

【译文分析】

①在新形势下,应巩固"中泰一家亲"的传统情谊,谱写"亲上加亲"的友好新篇章……

译文：Under the new circumstances，we need to cement the traditional ties of "Jeen Thai Phee Nong Gan" and write a new chapter of even closer friendship.

"中泰一家亲"的翻译可以应用泰语"Jeen Thai Phee Nong Gan"(中国 泰国 兄弟)进行直译,对于"亲上加亲"这个比喻可以省略不进行直译,而在表示友好关系的地方,用"close"的比较级"closer"进行意译。

②泰国盛产大米等农产品……

译文：Thailand is a main producer of rice and other agricultural products.

中文习惯用动词性表达方式:"盛产大米",而英文表达多用名词,所以在翻译成英文时可以转换词性,翻译成"a main producer of rice"。

2. 英译中

【原文】

Trade with China

① Premier Li Keqiang has described the UK and China as "indispensable partners". Prime Minister David Cameron has spoken of an open UK as the perfect partner for an opening China.

Our economic relationship is becoming much more important for both countries.

Two-way trade in 2014 was worth over $ 80 billion. UK goods exports continue to hit new heights，approaching £14 billion last year. That took us ahead of France to become the second largest European exporter to China，and made China our sixth most valuable export market.

Road vehicles are a major part of our export basket and China is rapidly becoming a vital market for UK automotive companies. Total UK automotive exports to China have grown five-fold over the last five years. Jaguar Land Rover (JLR) has been at the forefront. Companies such as Aston Martin，Lotus and Morgan are also doing more and more business. We want to see this relationship continue to grow.

We also see UK companies increasingly winning business in fast emerging new markets like health care.At the GREAT Festival, Shaw Health care, a UK elderly care provider signed a deal with a Chinese partner to deliver a boutique, high-end care facility on Shanghai's Bund.

②Oxford University also signed a deal with a local University that should unlock significant opportunities in the future.

The message that UKTI and CBBC need to get out is that China represents a huge opportunity as a trading partner for all UK based businesses, across a range of sectors.

This year UKTI will work with CBBC to organise a series of workshops across the UK targeting our medium sized businesses. The workshops will provide practical advice and assistance to encourage more UK companies to sell goods and services into China.

The first events will take place in London, Manchester and Scotland. We will be sending out invitations in due course, so watch this space.

China Outbound

The story on investment is even more striking. Chinese investment into the UK has risen by 85 percent, year on year, for the past five years. We are by far the most popular major European destination for investment from China.

Last year $5.1 billion of Chinese investment, nearly 30 percent of Europe's total, came to the UK. More and more Chinese companies are recognising the appeal of British brands and the attractions of the UK as a base for international business.

Look at Sanpower Group, which last year took control of House of Fraser Group. It now plans to open 50 Oriental Fraser stores across China.

Or NVC Lighting, which established UK headquarters in 2007 by purchasing a UK lighting company. Since 2009, it has grown at 30 percent a year and has used the UK as its base to reach out across Europe.

Chinese automotive companies like Changan, Shanghai Automotive Industry Corporation (SAIC) and Dynex have recognised that the UK has the automotive R&D capacities to propel them to the next level of technology and into international markets.

And the opportunity for Chinese companies to invest into the expanding UK Automotive supply chain has never been greater. UKTI has identified a ready market of £3 billion worth of components which could be manufactured in the UK.

Shandong Yongtai's investment into Covpress will likely be the first of what we hope will be many UK-Chinese supply chain partnerships that capitalise on this opportunity.

More to come

But there's potentially much more to come. We are only at the start of a long process of China's further integration into the global economy.

The Chinese economy may be 3 times larger than the UK economy but its stock of overseas investment is less than a third of the level of the UK's. At the APEC Summit in Beijing last year President Xi estimated that Chinese outward investment would exceed $ 1.25 trillion over the next 10 years.

A recent report by Pinsent Masons forecast that China is set to invest £ 105 billion in British infrastructure by 2025. Energy, property and transport are likely to be particularly popular. This year I hope we'll see more progress towards investment from China into the UK's civil nuclear power market, including final investment into the UK's first new civil nuclear project at Hinkley Point C.

We will continue to support China's interest in our highly competitive high speed rail market.

And I expect to see more interest in UK infrastructure and regeneration projects, building on previous investments in UK water companies, airports and real estate.

All across China there are companies with the resources and desire to invest overseas.

The CBBC, in partnership with UK Trade and Investment, can help them understand the UK investment environment and how to access opportunities here. And CBBC and UKTI can help connect them to our world leading financial and professional services sector, to take some of the risk out of their first steps in a new and unfamiliar market.

The UK welcomes Chinese investment, to help grow our economy and create jobs.

【译文】

对华贸易

①国务院总理李克强表示英国和中国是不可或缺的合作伙伴。首相戴维·卡梅伦同样表示开放的英国是开放的中国理想的合作伙伴。

两国的经济关系变得越来越重要。2014年双向贸易价值超过800亿美元。去年英国出口到中国的商品连续创新高,接近140亿英镑。这使我们超越法国成为中国在欧洲的第二大出口国,也使得中国成为我们的第六大出口市场。

汽车是我们主要的出口产品。而中国对于英国的汽车公司来说,正在迅速成为一个重要的市场。在过去的五年里,英国对中国汽车出口增长五倍。捷豹、路虎首当其冲。其他汽车品牌,比如阿斯顿马丁、莲花和摩根的出口也在增长。我们希望中英的关系越来越密切。

我们还看到英国公司不断在医疗等新兴市场领域赢取市场份额。在创意英伦盛典上,英国老年保健提供商 Shaw Healthcare 与中国合作伙伴签署了一项协议,该公司将在上海外滩提供高端精品保健设施。

②牛津大学也与中国一所大学签署了一项在未来会创造更多合作机会的协议。

英国贸易投资署和英中贸易协会想要传达的信息是,作为商业伙伴的中国对于英国各行各业来说意味着一个巨大的机会。

今年英国贸易投资署将会同英中贸易协会合作,在英国组织针对英国中型企业一系列的研讨会。研讨会将提供建议和帮助,鼓励更多的英国公司进入中国市场销售商品和服务。

第一轮研讨会活动将在伦敦、曼彻斯特和苏格兰进行。我们将适时发出邀请,所以请随时关注我们。

中国对外投资

中国对外投资的讯息更加引人注目。在过去的五年里,中国在英国的投资每年平均增长 85%。英国是最受中国投资者青睐的欧洲国家。

中国投资者去年在英国投资资金达到 51 亿美元,大约占中国在整个欧洲投资的30%。越来越多的中国公司将英国品牌的吸引力以及英国的吸引力看作国际商业合作的基础。

三胞集团在去年收购弗雷泽集团。它计划在中国开设 50 家东方弗雷泽商店。

雷士照明公司在 2007 年,通过收购一家英国的照明公司,在英国建立了总部。自2009 年以来,中国海外贸易投资以每年 30% 的速度增长,并且已经把英国作为海外贸易的基石,从而扩大中国在整个欧洲的投资范围。

中国汽车企业像长安、上海汽车工业集团总公司和丹尼克斯相信,英国的汽车研发能力可以帮助他们提高技术水平,进入国际市场。

对于吸引中国企业投资进入英国汽车供应链市场,机遇前所未有。英国贸易投资总署已初步确定有价值 30 亿英镑的零部件可以在英国生产。

我们希望山东永泰企业对英国考普莱公司的投资,将会带来英国和中国在供应链方面更多的合作案例。

更多商机

英中商贸还有更多机遇有待发现。目前这只是处于中国融入全球经济过程中的初步阶段。

中国经济规模大概是英国的三倍,但其海外投资尚不到英国的三分之一。去年,习近平主席在北京亚太经合组织峰会上预计中国的对外投资在未来10年内将超过1.25万亿美元。

品诚梅森律师事务所最近的一份报告预测指出,中国将在2025年以前向英国基础设施投资1050亿英镑。能源、房地产和交通领域可能会特别受欢迎。今年,我希望会有更多对英国民用核电市场的中国投资,包括投资英国欣克利角的新建民用核电站。

我们也将继续支持中国在英国高铁市场的投资。

除了在英国水务公司、机场和房地产方面的投资之外,我期待中国在英国基础设施和再生能源项目进行更多的合作。

在中国有很多掌握丰富资源的公司都迫切希望进行海外商业投资。

英中贸易协会和英国贸易投资署可以帮助他们了解英国的投资环境以及如何在英国获得发展机会。当中国企业在英国进行初步投资时,我们可以帮助这些企业与英国主要金融、专业服务部门联系以减轻企业的投资风险。

英国非常欢迎中国的投资者进入英国市场,助力英国经济增长和创造更多就业机会。

【译文分析】

① Premier Li Keqiang has described the UK and China as "indispensable partners". Prime Minister David Cameron has spoken of an open UK as the perfect partner for an opening China.

译文:国务院总理李克强表示英国和中国是不可或缺的合作伙伴。首相戴维·卡梅伦同样表示开放的英国是开放的中国理想的合作伙伴。

在此句的翻译当中,"perfect"一词如果只翻译成"伙伴",中文的意思不是很明确,因此在译成中文时需加上"合作"二字进行补充说明,使中文的意思更加明确。

②Oxford University also signed a deal with a local university that should unlock significant opportunities in the future.

译文:牛津大学也与中国一所大学签署了一项在未来会创造更多合作机会的协议。

英语中的定语从句大多后置,翻成中文,可以将定语从句按中文习惯前置,或者进行拆句,变成两个句子:"牛津大学也与中国一所大学签署了一项协议,这在未来会创造更多合作的机会。"

V. 技能训练之习语口译训练

口译主要通过口头上一种语言形式向另一种语言形式的转换,以实现跨文化、跨民族的交往与沟通。而习语能清晰地反映出一个民族的语言特色和文化特征,包含浓厚的民族色彩和地域特征。一般,中外领导人在外交场合交谈经常谈古论今、引经据典,古今中外都可能涉及,从而实现更好的交流与沟通。首先,译员应该明确哪些是习语。习语是"一种语言所特有的表达方式、语法结构、短语等,这种特定表达通过语言的使用而非语法或逻辑体现其含义"。习语严格意义上指的是成语,广义上还包括俗语、俚语、谚语、歇后语、典故等。其次,口译译员在翻译习语的过程中不但要认清语言各自的特点,也要注意它们之间的对应,在外国人引述中国习语时要能辨别出来。英汉习语的偶合现象在描写客观事物时较为明显,可以采取直译。例如,castle in the air(空中楼阁);as light as a feather(轻如鸿毛);like a bolt from the blue(晴天霹雳);add fuel to the flames(火上加油);strike while the iron is hot(趁热打铁)。

然而,就英汉习语而言,由于自然环境、风俗习惯、宗教信仰、思维方式、历史典故等方面的差异,英汉习语出现偶合现象相对较少,大多含有不同的意义和文化内涵。一味追求形式结构上的对应,很可能达不到"神似",并且导致误译。比较典型的例子是"Out of sight,out of mind"常常被误译为"眼不见,心不烦",其实它所指的是看不见了就容易忘,并没有烦恼的意思。另外一个例子是"Love me,love my dog"常被译为"爱屋及乌"。但是英文习语"Love me,love my dog"前半句是一个条件状语从句,后半句是祈使句,暗含如果你爱一个人,就应该接受这个人所爱的一切。在口语中,通常是由说话者向对方提出要求,而不是对方主动关爱自己。"爱屋及乌"则比喻爱一个人而连带地关心到与他/她有关的人或物。这种关心是自发的,并非被动。

译员在翻译习语时应充分理解习语所蕴涵的文化意义,并结合语境选择不同的翻译策略。一次记者招待会上总理用到了"喊破嗓子不如甩开膀子",译员张璐在进行翻译时巧妙地借用了英文中的"talk the talk"和"walk the walk"习语,通过归化策略将总理的这句话译为"Talking the talk is not as good as walking the walk",不仅形式上对等,还向外国媒体传达出我国政府改革的决心和意志。口译时,译员不仅要考虑译语的顺达,还要考虑习语背后的文化内涵,有时需要通过加注法补充必要的信息。对于中外习语的翻译,不仅要做到形似,还要做到神似这个技巧,需要日积月累的积淀,不能一蹴而就。

口译训练

Interpret the following idioms.

孤掌难鸣。

船到桥头自然直。

众人拾柴火焰高。

种瓜得瓜,种豆得豆。

志不立,天下无可成之事。

skate on thin ice

be (like) chalk and cheese

running on fumes

(just) a stone's throw

A miss is as good as a mile.

【参考译文】

孤掌难鸣。

译：A single bracelet does not jingle.

船到桥头自然直。

译：We'll cross that bridge when we come to it.

众人拾柴火焰高。

译：The bonfire burns higher when everyone adds firewood to it.

种瓜得瓜，种豆得豆。

译：You reap what you sow.

志不立，天下无可成之事。

译：Without strong determination，nothing can be accomplished.

skate on thin ice

译：如履薄冰

be（like）chalk and cheese

译：截然不同

running on fumes

译：精疲力竭

(just) a stone's throw

译：一箭之遥

A miss is as good as a mile.

译：错误再小也是错。

Ⅵ. 词汇拓展

承兑费 accepting charge

订单确认 acknowledgement of orders

实际负债 actual liability

追加费用 additional expense

预付款 advance payment

双边契约 bilateral contract

散货 bulk cargo

副本 carbon copy

现金购买 cash purchase

中央信托局 Central Trust of China

指定银行 chartered bank

信用证 letter of credit

商业利润 commercial profit

往来银行 correspondent bank

到期日 date due

延期付款 deferred payment

电汇 electronic transfer

出口配额 export quotas

外汇管制 foreign exchange control

销售总额 gross sales

参考文献

［1］肖忠华，戴光荣. 汉语译文中习语与词簇的使用特征：基于语料库的研究［J］. 外语研究，2010(3)：79-86.

［2］http：//www.fmprc.gov.cn/mfa_eng.

［3］http：//www.gov.cn/.

［4］http：//www.kekenet.com/kouyi/.

第七章　表演艺术

I. 词汇预习

backdrop［戏］背景幕布；背景；交流声

resonance 共鸣

bigwig 大人物

tael 两；银两

brothel 青楼

eunuch 太监，宦官

agate 玛瑙

disposition 性情，性格；意向，倾向；安排，配置

imagism 意象派

formality 拘泥形式；正式手续；例行公事；形式上的措施

cantabile 如歌的，轻柔流畅的

stuntman 特技替身演员

blockbuster 重磅炸弹，了不起的人或事；大片；风靡一时的事物

lconic 符号的；图标的；图符的；偶像的

wrench 猛拉；猛拽；（离别时的）痛苦，愁楚；扳钳；活动扳手

revelation［宗］天启，启示；揭发，暴露；意外的发现

nefarious 极坏的，恶毒的

supervillain 超级大反派，超级大坏蛋

infiltrate 渗透，（使）渗入；（使）潜入；渗透物

supremacist 至上主义者

extended-play record(EP)密纹唱片，迷你专辑

UNICEF 联合国儿童基金会

UNAIDS 联合国艾滋病联合规划署

Ⅱ. 典型句型

1. 中译英

(1) 中国的电影公司已不再满足于为好莱坞的影片搭设场景或提供临时演员,而是正在向价值链的上游移动,参与到世界级影片和动画长片的开发、设计和制作当中。

No longer content simply to build movie sets and provide extras in Hollywood films, Chinese studios are moving up the value chain, helping to develop, design and produce world-class films and animated features.

(2) 作为一门独立的表演艺术,中国舞蹈发展到明(1368—1644)、清(1616—1911)呈衰落趋势。

As an independent art form, Chinese dance declined in the Ming (1368—1644) and Qing (1616—1911) dynasties.

(3) 要抖威风,跟洋人干去,洋人厉害! 英法联军烧了圆明园,尊家吃着官饷,可没见您去冲锋打仗!

Sounds like you are a powerful man, then why don't you fight against the invaders? The British and French troops fired the Imperial Summer Palace, and you taking official rates, were seen nowhere in the battle fields.

(4) 薛之谦称他做音乐是出于对它的热爱,而不是为了钱。去年,他发行了一张名为《绅士》的迷你专辑,其中共收录了三首他创作的歌曲。

Xue Zhiqian claims that he creates music purely out of love, not for money. Last year, he released an EP called *Gentleman*, featuring three songs he wrote.

(5) 作为中国的文化瑰宝,唐三彩必将获得全中国和全世界人民越来越多的欣赏和喜爱。

Being a great treasure of the Chinese culture, Tang Sancai ceramics will surely be more and more appreciated by people in China and in the whole world.

2. 英译中

(1) The song, called So Far, the Sofa Is So Far, uses daily life in Beijing as a backdrop for complaints about overtime work among office workers.

这首歌名为《感觉身体被掏空》,以北京的日常生活为背景,描绘了上班族对加班的抱怨。

(2) Albus Dumbledore is one of the best characters from the whole series! But did you know that two actors played Dumbledore? Michael Gambon played the character from *Prisoner of Azkaban* until the end.

邓布利多校长是整个系列中最受欢迎的角色之一,但你有发现他是由两位演员扮演的吗?迈克尔·甘本是从《哈利·波特与阿兹卡班囚徒》才开始饰演校长,直到最后一部。

(3) The singer-songwriter tops *Forbes*' annual list of the 100 highest-paid celebrities with $170 million.

这位创作型歌手以 1.7 亿美元的收入高居《福布斯》年度艺人收入百强榜首。

(4) Chopin's incredible talent was apparent at a young age.

肖邦的惊人才华在他很小的时候便展露无遗。

(5) Music makes everything have more emotional resonance. Let's see how it does for this talk. The right piece of music at the right time fuses with us on a cellular level.

音乐让一切事物拥有更多的情感共鸣。让我们看看它对这次演讲的效果如何。在适当的时机,恰到好处的音乐片段会在身体的深处与我们融为一体。

Ⅲ. 对话翻译

刘麻子:说说吧,十两银子行不行?你说干脆的!我忙,没工夫专伺候你!

(Liu: Give me a reply, if ten taels of silver is OK with you? Time is running out. I'm busy and couldn't waste any more time on you.)

康六:刘爷!十五岁的大姑娘,就值十两银子吗?

(Kang: Milord, how can a 15-year-old girl be worth just ten taels?)

刘麻子:卖到窑子去,也许多拿一两八钱的,可是你又不肯!

(Liu: Of course worth more if sold to the brothels. The point is you don't allow that.)

康六:那是我的亲女儿!我能够……

(Kang: That's my own daughter, how can I...)

刘麻子:有女儿,你可养活不起,这怪谁呢?

(Liu: Who is to blame if you cannot raise your own daughter?)

康六:那不是因为乡下种地的都没法子混了吗?一家大小要是一天能吃上一顿粥,我要还想卖女儿,我就不是人!

(Kang: We live with the land in the countryside but couldn't feed ourselves. If only we had plain porridge each meal, I would not sell my daughter or I'm heartless...)

刘麻子:那是你们乡下的事,我管不着。我受你之托,教你不吃亏,又教你女儿有个吃饱饭的地方,这还不好吗?

(Liu: That's your business. I'm honest to you and can get your daughter a place where she can eat her fill.)

康六：到底给谁呢？

(Kang：Who on earth is pursuing her?)

刘麻子：我一说，你必定从心眼里乐意！一位在宫里当差的！

(Liu：I promise you will be satisfied! He serves the Emperor in the Palace. It can only be your daughter's fate which leads her to such a bigwig.)

康六：宫里当差的谁要个乡下丫头呢？

(Kang：Who is that man in the Palace needing a country girl?)

刘麻子：庞总管！你也听说过庞总管吧？伺候着太后，红得不得了，连家里打醋的瓶子都是玛瑙的！

(Liu：Eunuch Pang! You must know him；he is the favorite of the Queen Mother. Even the vinegar bottle in his home is made of agate!)

康六：刘大爷，把女儿给太监作老婆，我怎么对得起人呢？

(Kang：Milord, it doesn't make sense to marry my daughter to a eunuch.)

刘麻子：卖女儿，无论怎么卖，也对不起女儿！你糊涂！你看，姑娘一过门，吃的是珍馐美味，穿的是绫罗绸缎，这不是造化吗？怎样，摇头不算点头算，来个干脆的！

(Liu：Think about your daughter，it's quite fair to her. When she is married，both of the food and clothes she have will be the best. What a good fortune it is. Come on，let's make it done.)

康六：真荒诞，哪有……他就给十两银子？

(Kang：How absurd... Does he only afford ten taels of silver?)

刘麻子：找遍了你们全村儿，找得出十两银子找不出？在乡下，五斤白面就换个孩子，你不是不知道！

(Liu：You know that. It's impossible to find that money even if you dig through your village. Be grateful，it is the public secret there that two kilograms of flour exchanges a child.)

康六：我，唉！我得跟姑娘商量一下！

(Kang：I have to persuade my poor daughter.)

刘麻子：告诉你，过了这个村可没有这个店，耽误了事可别怨我！快去快来！

(Liu：Tell you what? Chance doesn't always wait for you. Don't regret after missing it.)

康六：唉！我一会儿就回来！

(Kang：I'll be back soon.)

Ⅳ. 篇章翻译

1. 中译英

【原文】

如何拍摄一部不可能完成的电影

我拍摄了一部不可能完成的电影,但是在一开始我并不知道有这么大的难度,不过,也正是因为不知道,我才得以完成这部影片。

《三月和四月》是一部科幻电影。故事发生在 50 年之后的蒙特利尔。以前没有人在魁北克拍摄过这样的电影,因为成本高,故事又发生在未来,而且有大量的特效,需要用绿屏拍摄。然而我从童年看漫画书和憧憬未来的时候开始就想拍摄一部这样的电影。

美国制作人看到这部电影时,他们以为我有很高的预算,大概 2300 万元。然而事实上我的预算只有这个数字的十分之一。我用 230 万元就拍摄了《三月和四月》。

①你可能会想,这是怎么回事?我是怎么做到的?有两个因素不可或缺,第一是时间。如果没有钱,就只能慢慢来了,我花了 7 年时间才完成《三月和四月》。第二是对电影的热爱。所有参与这部影片制作的人对我都非常慷慨。每个部门似乎都一贫如洗,所以我们只能依靠自己的创造力将遇到的每一个问题转化为机会。

事实上,这也就是我今天演讲的中心:限制,人在创作时面临严重限制的时候,反倒可以激发人的创造力。

不过,请允许我说一说往事。我 20 出头的时候出版过一些图文小说,它们和一般的图文小说不同,是用图片和文字讲述科幻故事的书,参与电影改编的演员大多参与过图文小说的创作。他们以一种实验性的、戏剧性的、简单的方式扮演不同的人物。

演员之一是优秀的舞台导演和演员,他叫 Robert Lepage。我非常喜欢他,我从小就非常喜欢他。②我很欣赏崇拜他的演艺事业,我希望他能参与我的疯狂项目。他非常善良,愿意放下自己的形象去演绎 Eugène Spaak 这个角色。Eugène Spaak 是一位在时间、空间、爱、音乐和女性中间寻找关联的宇宙学家和艺术家。他是诠释这个角色的完美人选。事实上,Robert 也是最早给我机会的人。他信任我、鼓励我,让我把我的书改编为一部电影并且自己做电影的编剧、导演和制片人。

事实上,Robert 参演这部电影的方式是限制激发创意的第一个例子。因为他是世界上最忙的人。他的工作日程已经排到 2042 年了,想跟他取得联系很难,而我希望他参演电影,在电影中再度演绎他的角色。但是问题是,如果我等到 2042 年,我的电影就不是发生在未来的科幻电影了。我不能这么做,这是一个很严峻的问题。怎么才能让一个超级大忙人来参演电影呢?

我在一次制作会议上半开玩笑地说——顺便一提,这是真的——我说:"要不然我们把他变成全息图吧"? 因为这个角色难觅踪迹又无所不在,在我脑海中他是一个发光的生物,他身处现实和虚拟世界之间,所以用全息影像塑造这个角色非常合理。

所有坐在桌边的人都笑了,但是这个玩笑是个不错的想法,所以我们最后真的实践了这个想法。

【译文】

How I Made an Impossible Film

I made a film that was impossible to make,but I didn't know it was impossible,and that's how I was able to do it.

Mars et Avil is a science fiction film. It's set in Montreal some 50 years in the future. No one had done that kind of movie in Quebec before because it's expensive,it's set in the future,and it's got tons of visual effects,and it's shot on green screen. Yet this is the kind of movie that I wanted to make ever since I was a kid,really,back when I was reading some comic books and dreaming about what the future might be.

When American producers see my film,they think that I had a big budget to do it,like 23 million. But in fact I had 10 percent of that budget. I did *Mars et Avril* for only 2.3 million.

①So you might wonder what's the deal here. How did I do this? Well,it's two things. First,it's time. When you don't have money,you must take time,and it took me seven years to do *Mars et Avril*. The second aspect is love. I got tons and tons of generosity from everyone involved. And it seems like every department had nothing,so they had to rely on our creativity and turn every problem into an opportunity.

And that brings me to the point of my talk,actually,how constraints,big creative constraints,can boost creativity.

But let me go back in time a bit. In my early 20s,I did some graphic novels,but they weren't your usual graphic novels. They were books telling a science fiction story through images and text,and most of the actors who are now starring in the movie adaptation were already involved in these books portraying characters into a sort of experimental,theatrical,simplistic way.

And one of these actors is the great stage director and actor Robert Lepage. And I just love this guy. I've been in love with this guy since I was a kid. ②His career I admire a lot. And I wanted this guy to be involved in my crazy project,and he was kind enough to lend his image to the character of Eugène Spaak,who is a cosmologist and artist who seeks relation in between time,space,love,music and women. And he was a perfect fit for the part, and Robert is actually the one who gave me my first chance. He was the one who believed in me and encouraged me to do an adaptation of my books into a film, and to write, direct, and produce the film myself.

And Robert is actually the very first example of how constraints can boost creativity. Because this guy is the busiest man on the planet. I mean, his agenda is booked until 2042, and he's really hard to get, and I wanted him to be in the movie, to reprise his role in the movie. But the thing is, had I waited for him until 2042, my film wouldn't be a futuristic film any more, so I just couldn't do that. Right? But that's kind of a big problem. How do you get somebody who is too busy to star in a movie?

Well, I said as a joke in a production meeting—and this is a true story, by the way—I said, "Why don't we turn this guy into a hologram? Because, you know, he is everywhere and nowhere on the planet at the same time, and he's an illuminated being in my mind, and he's in between reality and virtual reality, so it would make perfect sense to turn this guy into a hologram."

Everybody around the table laughed, but the joke was kind of a good solution, so that's what we ended up doing.

【译文分析】

①你可能会想，这是怎么回事？我是怎么做到的？

译文：So you might wonder what's the deal here. How did I do this?

在演讲和会议翻译中经常会出现类似的设问句，译者要注意语气的随和性和句型的简单性，在中文中体会到的设问要在同样的英文句中得到表现。同时注意多方面运用情态动词，改变语气。

②我很欣赏崇拜他的演艺事业，我希望他能参与我的疯狂项目。他非常善良，愿意放下自己的形象去演绎 Eugène Spaak 这个角色。Eugène Spaak 是一位在时间、空间、爱、音乐和女性中间寻找关联的宇宙学家和艺术家。

译文：His career I admire a lot. And I wanted this guy to be involved in my crazy project, and he was kind enough to lend his image to the character of Eugène Spaak, who is a cosmologist and artist who seeks relation in between time, space, love, music and women.

这个句子的复杂在于其合并性，其中的"他""项目""角色"都出现重叠。在译"放下自己的形象"时使用了"lend"这个词，就非常恰当，也很好地表现了该演员对表演的奉献。另外，该句有很长的前置修饰语，在英文中转换成为后置修饰，也是语言习惯所致。

2. 英译中

【原文】

The blockbuster success of *Captain America：Civil War* confirms it：Captain America is one of the most iconic superheroes in the Marvel Universe. That's true on the comics' side as well as the movies，and this week brings the first issue of *Captain America：Steve Rogers*，the series that returns Steve Rogers to his youth and vigor after spending some time as a de-superpowered old man. Sam Wilson (the Falcon) had been filling in as Captain America，but it's safe to say fans are excited to see the original character back.

Too bad Marvel decided to throw a wrench in all of that.

Captain America：Steve Rogers ♯1，out today，ends with the revelation that Steve Rogers is，and has always been，an undercover operative for the nefarious organization Hydra. Writer Nick Spencer and Marvel editor Tom Brevoort spoke with *Entertainment Weekly*(*EW*) about the genesis of this twist，what it means for Sam Wilson，and emphasized that yes，this really is Steve Rogers.

That's right，the most recognizable superhero in the Marvel Universe is actually a supervillain. Here goes something.

EW：How long has this been in development? What inspired you to rethink such an iconic character in this way?

BREVOORT：It made something new and unexpected out of restoring Steve to youth and vigor. ① Nobody was especially surprised that Steve got restored，but hopefully readers will be surprised by this revelation—and by the stories that follow on from this point.

SPENCER：Rick Remender，who was the previous writer on Captain America，had been building towards this story of Hydra having infiltrated various institutions of government and various super teams. I thought that sounded like too big of a story. I drilled it down and thought，what if there's just one very valuable Hydra plant? What if they're looking for 100 people，but there's just one? So I started asking，who's the worst person it could possibly be? It was really obvious straight away that there's nobody who could do more damage and nobody that could be a more valuable Hydra plant than Steve Rogers. That was really the genesis. It sprang pretty organically from story ideas that were already on the table.

EW：Issue 1 lays the groundwork for the reveal with flashbacks to Steve's childhood and his first contact with an operative of Hydra. Does this mean it's been this way his whole life?

BREVOORT: Well, No. 2 rolls back the clock a little bit to further illuminate where Steve's head is at and how he got this way. And from there, the story will get larger over the course of time than you probably imagine that it can.

SPENCER: Issue 2 will lay a lot of our cards on the table in terms of what the new status quo is, but the one thing we can say unequivocally is: This is not a clone, not an imposter, not mind control, not someone else acting through Steve. This really is Steve Rogers, Captain America himself.

EW: What does it mean for the Marvel Universe to have its most iconic superhero flip sides like this?

BREVOORT: Well, it puts the readers one step ahead of most of the characters in the Marvel Universe, so that, in Hitchcock tradition, they're aware that the most trusted and most respected superhero within the Marvel Universe is now a wolf among the flock, who could strike at any time.

SPENCER: Captain America is not just one of the most recognizable faces in the Marvel Universe. He's an inspiring figure, somebody who brings people together. Everybody here obviously gets that. What you hope is that this story, in its own very different way, highlights those things and only continues to elevate the character in importance, and only serves to illustrate how powerful that symbol is.

EW: Sam Wilson is nowhere to be seen here. What can you tease about his role in this story going forward?

SPENCER: Obviously this is going to change everybody's perception of Sam's situation. When Steve came back to youth and full vigor, people worried about Sam's solvency, they worried about his relevance, and I got to just sit and grin while everybody was doing that. It goes without saying that this is going to have a profound impact on Sam's story and Sam's life. He's about to be put through the ringer in a way we rarely see with a character. He's going to be challenged in fundamental ways. Sam is a huge part of what we have planned.

EW: This issue also introduces us to a new generation of Hydra fighters, who resemble white supremacist organizations. What were your influences there?

SPENCER: That's exactly right. Those are the two things that are being conflated here to some extent. The Red Skull obviously has a lot of experience with fascism and Nazism and white supremacy movements. What we're seeing here is an adoption of modern-day terror tactics. For me, those were an interesting couple of components to put together. ② What we see throughout the world right now is that these kinds of movements are heavily resurgent and record-breaking recruitment numbers. So some of this is trying to be a little forward-thinking in picturing what the world might look like if these kinds of organizations decide to adopt these kinds of tactics.

【译文】

热门电影《美国队长：内战》用巨高的票房胜利力证了美国队长这一角色是漫威宇宙中最受欢迎的形象之一。这一点在漫画和电影中都得到了证实。本周，在最新一期美国队长系列漫画《美国队长：史蒂夫·罗杰斯》中，被剥夺超级血清并衰老的史蒂夫·罗杰斯重返青春并重获能力。山姆·威尔逊（即猎鹰）曾代替史蒂夫成为美国队长，不过据可靠消息，读者更喜欢原本的美国队长。

悲催的是，漫威决心把这一切都搞黄。

今日发行的《美国队长：史蒂夫·罗杰斯》第一话的结尾揭露，史蒂夫·罗杰斯一直以来都是邪恶组织九头蛇安插的卧底。美队漫画作者尼克·斯宾塞、漫威高级副总裁汤姆·布雷武特做客《娱乐周刊》，讨论这次反转的意义所在，以及对于山姆·威尔逊意味着什么。两位还着重强调，这确实是队长本人。

就是这样，漫威宇宙中最具标志性的英雄人物真身是一位超级反派。这可真有意思了。

《娱乐周刊》：你们对这个情节计划了多久？你们是从哪里获得的灵感这样重塑这个经典角色？

布雷武特：史蒂夫·罗杰斯的重获青春与力量，带来了很多既新鲜又出乎意料的东西。①没人会意外队长的重现，但是他们肯定会因为这次剧情反转以及后续的情节而大吃一惊。

斯宾塞：美国队长的前作者瑞克·瑞曼德构建美国队长的故事时，设计了众多九头蛇渗入各种政府部门以及超级团队之中的情节。我们觉得这个情节对这个故事来说，太庞大了。我们深度探讨了这个情节设置，然后考虑，如果只有一个九头蛇的超级卧底会怎样呢？要是他们一直以为自己在寻找 100 个人，结果却只有一个呢？所以，我就开始问了，谁能是最坏的那个人呢？很明显，没有任何一个角色黑化带来的反差、造成的破坏、产生的价值能超过美国队长就是九头蛇安插的卧底。这个情节就是这么来的。它源于原本的美国队长系列情节，又自行其道。

《娱乐周刊》：第一话中呈现出了史蒂夫的童年时期以及他最初与九头蛇关键人物接触的一系列情节铺垫。这是否意味着接下来他的一生都将遵循这一主线？

布雷武特：是的，第二话中我们会将时间轴往回推，进一步呈现出史蒂夫这一角色的源头以及他是如何走上这条道路的。从那里开始，这个故事推进的时间长度会远远超出读者们的想象。

斯宾塞：第二话中我们会就新情节进行进一步的讨论，不过，有一点是毫无疑问的：那就是，没有克隆，没有冒名顶替，没有思想控制，没有别人通过史蒂夫施展手段。超级反派就是史蒂夫·罗杰斯，就是美国队长本人。

《娱乐周刊》：最具标志性的英雄反水对整个漫威宇宙来说意味着什么呢？

布雷武特：现在读者们在这件事上已经领先了绝大多数的漫威英雄，类似于希区柯克的风格，就是让读者们先行意识到他们最为信任和尊重的英雄其实是一只披着羊皮隐藏在羊群里的恶狼，随时可能撕开伪善的伪装。

斯宾塞：美国队长不仅是漫威宇宙最具辨识度的英雄之一，他还是一个鼓舞人心的精神领袖，他把人们团结在一起，这是每个人都知道的。你们可以期望的是这个故事会用非常与众不同的方式继续突出这一点，并进一步地提升这个角色的重要性，以此来说明这个具有象征意义的形象所拥有的力量。

《娱乐周刊》：至此山姆·威尔逊还不见踪迹，你们可以谈谈他将在这个故事的发展中起到的作用吗？

斯宾塞：显然这会让所有人对山姆的印象有所改观。当史蒂夫重回年轻状态时，人们曾经担心过山姆的偿债能力和恰当性，我基本是看看笑笑。毫无疑问这会对山姆的故事和生活产生深远的影响。他将以一种很少在别的角色上出现过的方式陷入困境，他会面临巨大的挑战。山姆本来就是我们计划中的重要部分。

《娱乐周刊》：这一期还向我们介绍了新一代的九头蛇战士，他们感觉上有些类似于白人至上主义者组织。请问是否是受到这些组织的影响？

斯宾塞：的确是这样，其实在某种程度上更像是两者的结合。红骷髅在很多行动上显然有法西斯主义、纳粹主义和白人至上运动的影子。而在这一期里我们看到的是现代的恐怖主义战略。对于我来说，是将这两种元素结合在一起。②如今放眼世界，我们看到的是此类运动的大量复苏，参与的人数也正在打破纪录。所以这其实也是一种前瞻性的设想，是向人们呈现出当这些恐怖组织决定采取类似的恐怖战略时，这个世界可能的模样。

【译文分析】

①Nobody was especially surprised that Steve got restored, but hopefully readers will be surprised by this revelation——and by the stories that follow on from this point.

译文：没人会意外队长的重现，但是他们肯定会因为这次剧情反转以及后续的情节而大吃一惊。

Steve 是美国队长的名字，有时听众更习惯于听到他被称呼为队长，而不是译为中文名字"史蒂夫"。对于副词"especially"的翻译也是采用非一一对应的手法，直接译入"意外"的词意比较自然。对于两次出现的介词"by"采用了合并手法，没有突出被动意义。

②What we see throughout the world right now is that these kinds of movements are heavily resurgent and record-breaking recruitment numbers.

译文：如今放眼世界，我们看到的是此类运动的大量复苏，参与的人数也正在打破纪录。

从句作主语的时候，口译要注意调整为汉语习惯的语序，同样的情况还有动名词和动词不定式作主语，因为汉语习惯中大多为人物作主语，所以可以忽略"what"这个引导词。英语中很多"record-breaking"之类的合成词充当形容词的作用，而在口译时转化为"打破纪录"更符合中文中的动宾结构，视为形容词转换为动词的译法。

Ⅴ. 口译技能训练之临场应变

口译，是一种通过听取和解析源语所表达的信息，随即将其转译为目标语语言符号，进而达到传递信息之目的的言语交际活动。它是一种即时性很强的语言交际活动。为了保证交际双方信息的表达及信息的接收能够连续、顺畅地进行，口译员必须在很短的时间内顺畅、快速地完成转换信息的任务。为了做到这一点，口译员必须具备良好的临场应变能力和掌握一些应变策略。

口译中的应变策略指的是译者能够在不影响源语主要信息，不影响说话者主要意图的基础上，适当地对源语进行调整，适当地处理好源语中的难点，使其更符合当时当地的情形和场合，并使交际顺利地进行。口译种类繁多，要想找到一种"放之四海而皆准"的策略简直不可能。下面为口译中常见的几种应变策略。

1. 化繁为简策略

化繁为简策略，即在不影响源语主要信息传达的基础上对源语中出现的无法用目标语处理的材料或技术性较强的材料，在直接译入到目标语中很难被目标语听众所理解的情况下而简化、概述、省略、解释源语信息的一种翻译策略。

例 1：2100 万台湾同胞都是中国人，都是骨肉同胞、手足兄弟。

译文：The 21 million compatriots in Taiwan are all Chinese and our own flesh and blood.

"骨肉同胞"与"手足兄弟"意义重复，故翻译时删去"手足兄弟"（或"骨肉同胞"）。在形式上也要养成习惯积累尽可能简短的表达方式。

例 2：古中华文明的起源和发展过程是考古学家和历史学家探索的重要课题。

例 2 的"考古学家和历史学家"（archeologists and historians）对口译员来说可能一下子反应不过来，可概括译为 experts，基本不影响上下文意思的连贯。

例 3：加拿大为老年人、残疾人、病人和失业者制定了一项综合社会保险计划。

例 3 的"老年人、残疾人、病人和失业者"字面上直译为"the aged, the disabled, the

sick and the unemployed"。若出现笔记不全，个别用词有所犹豫时，口译员可大胆地用"the unemployed and the other disadvantaged（groups）"来进行归纳，保全整个句子大意的畅通。

例 4：我要提的问题是环境污染问题。我们知道今天中国是一个非常具有科技基础的国家，我所知道的每天现在制造的垃圾，当然我的发音不一定标准，有 17857 公吨；第二，每人每天有 4757 公斤……总理先生，你想一想，你将来的丰功伟绩可能就化为乌有了。这是我的问题，谢谢。

译文：I have a question on the environmental pollution. We know that China is already a country with a very solid foundation in terms of science and technology. It is said that large amount of rubbish has been created every day in this country according to my statistics and that everyday about seventeen thousand eight hundred and fifty seven metric tons of rubbish is being created in this country... Probably your achievements at the end of the term of office will be compromised. Thank you.

这是台湾新闻通讯社记者在十届全国人大四次会议记者招待会上对温家宝总理的提问。由于这位记者的中文说得很不好，出现了非常明显的语法错误。在口译过程中，口译者自然地省去了一些意义不大的和错误的语句，如："第二个""我的发音不一定标准""你想一想""这是我的问题""每人每天有 4757 公斤"。错误的句子会造成听者理解上的障碍。为了准确地传达说话者的意思，译者可以适当删除一些不必要的和影响理解的语句。

2. "洋"为"中"用策略

借用目标语中现成的表达法来替代源语信息。

有一位译者在陪同外国友人游玩时，恰逢国人祭祖。看到路上来来往往的扫墓者，友人问译者："Are they celebrating a special day here?"。出于情急，译者一时想不起贴切的译文，便灵机一动，说"It's the 'Memorial Day' for Chinese people to worship their ancestors."起到应急之用（"Memorial Day"指美国大多数州的阵亡将士纪念日）。

3. 言内明示（增译）策略

口译中要将源语的内涵和外延，及其所包含的文化信息用明明白白的语言表达出来。

比如，在介绍美国电子商务的发展态势时，一位 IT 人士谈道："The current ecommerce landscape features a number of important guideposts that can help direct the innovative garage dreamer down a feasible path to success."。在这句话中，garage dreamer 对于一个不熟悉电子商务发展历程的译者而言，是一个无法逾越的鸿沟。我们知道，电子商务亿万富翁在创业之初，往往由于手头拮据，资金不足，只能勉强在旧车库（garage）里创业，但他们对未来都充满了憧憬和幻想（dream），也正因为如此，他们中许多人才脱颖而出，取得了非凡的成就。

有了这一层文化语境（cultural situation）的知识，问题自然迎刃而解。因此，在译文"目前的电子商务发展态势有几个重要的特征：它们将为颇具创新精神的'车库幻想家'指明一条成功之路"加上一句，"所谓 garage dreamer（车库幻想家）指的就是那些'从车库里发家的电子商务巨头'"。

Ⅵ. 词汇拓展

临时演员 extras

票房 box office

盗版问题 piracy

期待已久 long-awaited

令人震撼 breathtaking

平淡的对话 flat dialogue

故事情节 storyline

员工 personnel

导演 director

编舞者 choreographer

动画长片 animated features

创意过程 creative process

制作队 production team

执行制作人 executive producer

音乐总监 musical director

技术总监 technical director

舞台设计师 stage designer

道具负责人 production property master

音响设计师 sound designer

服装设计师 costume designer

编外演员 supernumerary

丑角 joker

乐团 orchestra

音乐指挥 music conductor

司仪 master of ceremony

双复演员 double cast

后台人员 backstage crew

道具人员 property crew

化妆师 makeup artist

跑腿 gopher

参考文献

[1] 梅德明.上海市口译资格证书考试高级口译教程[M].上海：上海外语教育出版社,1996.

[2] 老舍.茶馆(汉英对照)[M].霍华译.北京：外文出版社,2001.

[3] 王金波,王燕.从信息论的角度看汉英翻译的冗余现象[J].中国科技翻译,2002,15(4)：1-4.

[4] 王绍祥.口译应变策略[J].中国科技翻译,2004(1)：19-22.

[5] 叶志良.戏剧鉴赏[M].北京：外语教学与研究出版社,2009.

[6] http：//bj.xdf.cn/publish/portal24/tab16999/info752051.htm.

[7] http：//www.hxen.com/englisharticle/yingyuyuedu/2016-07-30/437910.html.

[8] http：//www.kekenet.com/kouyi/.

[9] http：//www.yeeworld.com.

[10] http：//www.ted.com/talks.

第八章 社交媒体

I. 词汇预习

by some counts 根据某些数据统计

live social streaming 社交流媒体直播

early adopter 早期用户

active user 活跃用户

live streaming 流媒体直播

following 跟随者

broadcast live video 进行视频直播

on a constant basis 持续不断地

mutual follow 相互关注

Direct Messages(DM)私密消息

ditch 取消

close the gap 弥补差距

unveiled or upgraded 推出或升级

in-line buy buttons 内置的"购买"功能

workplace productivity tool 职场效率工具

similar transformations 类似的转型

infidelity 不忠

a similar proportion 类似比例

former partners 前任

during a pilot phase 在试验阶段

senior users 高级会员

drop the cap 取消上限

self-deprecating attitude 自嘲的态度

professional opportunities and pitfalls 职业机会和陷阱

Ⅱ. 典型句型

1. 英译中

（1）With everyone from your boss to your competitors and everyone in between checking your LinkedIn profile，Twitter feed and Facebook page on a constant basis，there is a lot of pressure to promote yourself.

现在，从你的老板到竞争对手，以及其他许多人，都在持续不断地查看你的领英个人资料、推特信息和脸书页面，因此，自我推销要面临巨大的压力。

（2）Twitter ditched the "mutual follow" requirement for its DM（Direct Messages）feature，meaning companies and customers can now contact each other directly and privately.

推特取消了发送私密消息必须首先"相互关注"的要求，意味着企业和消费者现在可以直接进行私密交流了。

（3）In 2016，expect to see social media training finally begin to make its way into the workplace in an effort to close this gap—similar to initiatives launched when office software suites and later email and the Internet itself emerged as critical business tools.

2016 年，我们有望看到一些企业为弥补这些差距而着手开展社交媒体技能培训——就好像当年的微软办公套件和后来的电子邮件刚刚成为企业的重要工具时一样。

（4）Social shopping takes off：Over the last year，Twitter，Facebook，Instagram and Pinterest all unveiled or upgraded in-line buy buttons，which allow users to purchase clothes，crafts，gadgets and more without ever leaving their feeds.

社交购物广泛普及：过去一年中，推特、脸书、照片分享和品趣志等主流社交网络都推出或升级了应用内置的"购买"功能，使用户可以在应用内直接购买衣服、工艺品和其他一些小玩意儿。

（5）Facebook isn't just about connecting with friends：It's now（or soon to be）a workplace productivity tool，a video sharing and streaming platform，a place to shop，etc. Similar transformations can be seen across LinkedIn，Instagram，Pinterest and Snapchat，among other networks.

脸书也不止是要把你与好友们联系起来，它现在已经成为（或即将成为）一个职场效率工具，一个视频分享和流媒体平台，一家自由购物的电商。领英、照片分享、品趣志和阅后即焚等社交网站，也在进行类似的转型。

2. 中译英

（1）2015 年见证了社交流媒体直播的诞生，"潜望镜"和蒙哥等应用已经赢得了不少早期用户。

2015 saw the birth of live social streaming，with apps like Periscope and Meerkat winning over early adopters.

（2）视频服务也在各大社交网络上发展得风生水起，脸书用户的每日视频点击量达到 80 亿次（根据某些数据统计，甚至超过了油管）。

Video dominated social headlines，with Facebook users now logging an estimated 8 billion video views a day（even more than on YouTube，by some counts）.

（3）如果发个微博就能很快获得回复，为什么还要排队打热线电话呢？但现实却是另一番情景。

Why wait on the phone when you can Tweet and get an answer immediately? But the reality has been quite different.

（4）夏末，推特旗下的"潜望镜"公司已拥有 1000 万名活跃用户，本月还被苹果评为 2015 年最佳苹果应用。

By late summer，Twitter-owned Periscope already boasted 10 million active users，and just this month it was named by Apple the best iOS App of 2015.

（5）脸书直播将使流媒体直播成为主流：2015 年，一批流媒体直播应用的诞生给人们带来了不小的惊喜，它们使用户可以对粉丝进行视频直播。

Facebook Live makes live streaming mainstream：2015 started off with lots of excitement about the new crop of live streaming apps，which allow users to broadcast live video to their followings.

Ⅲ. 段落翻译

1. 中译英

【原文】

中国最流行的微博平台——新浪微博，正在取消它的字母、数字和符号字数的上限，意味着微博会员可以写长博文了。到现在为止，这个网络社交平台仍然受 140 个字符的限制。报道说，在试验阶段，用户信息流里仍会保持只显示前 140 字，但用户可以点击"全文"查看全部信息。报道还补充说，只有"高级会员"能在 1 月 28 日使用字数扩展功能，不过在 2 月底，该功能将对所有微博用户开放。在新浪公司最新的账务报告里，它称微博用户已达 2 亿多人。

【译文】

Sina Weibo-China's most popular micro—blogging platform—is dropping its cap on the number of letters，numbers and symbols Its members can write in a single post.

Until now，the social network had been defined by its 140-character limit. It said that during a pilot phase，only the first 140 characters would be shown to readers up front and they would have to click on a link to see the contents of longer messages. It added that only "senior users" would be able to use the extended facility from the start but it would be open to other members before the end of February. In its last financial report，Sina Corp said its Weibo service had more than 200 million users.

2. 英译中

【原文】

Facebook and Twitter have become a significant threat to marriage—with social media now a factor in an increasing number of divorce cases，say lawyers. One in seven married individuals have considered divorce because of their spouse's postings of Facebook or other online sites，according to research. A similar proportion admit that they search online for evidence of their partner's infidelity，while nearly one in five say they have daily rows because of the way their husband or wife uses social media. The research was commissioned by law firm Slater and Gordon in response to an increase in the number of its clients who said that Facebook，Skype，Snapchat，Twitter，What'sApp or other social media sites had played a part in their divorce.

【译文】

律师称,在越来越多的离婚案件中,脸书和推特等社交媒体已成为严重威胁婚姻存续的一个因素。根据研究,七分之一的已婚人士曾因配偶发在脸书或其他网站上的帖子考虑过离婚。类似比例的人承认,他们曾在网上寻找伴侣不忠的证据;近五分之一的人表示,夫妻二人每天都会因为彼此在社交媒体上的所作所为而吵架。该研究是由斯莱特和戈登律师事务所委托相关机构做出的。斯莱特和戈登律师事务所发现越来越多的客户声称,他们之所以离婚,与脸书、Skype、阅后即焚、推特和What'sApp等社交媒体有很大关系,于是该律所发起了这个调查。

Ⅳ. 篇章翻译

1. 中译英

【原文】

动图,第三种语言

何苦绞尽脑汁用沉闷的文字在社交媒体上发评论？亦或是发用过无数次的表情？快来试试动图(图形交换格式的简称)吧,它能让你的社交互动更有趣。

动图是一种流行文化现象。简单说来它们就是动态的图片,循环交替以取得最佳效果。《纽约时报》甚至预言动态图会成为传递信息的"第三种语言"。现在每 24 小时脸书的通信程序都会传输 500 多万张动态图。

①由于移动通信技术的进步和大量通信程序的开发，动图"已经成为一种主流的数字化表达，它通过非文字甚至非图片的方式传递着人类复杂的情绪和想法"，《纽约时报》评论道。"年轻人引领了动图潮流，因为使用动图能更好地展现他们的网络个性，"美国社交网站"微博客"编辑主任托弗尔·克里斯告诉美国公共广播公司。

动图还成了观察美国名人文化的窗口。流行歌手和电影明星的图片被做成动图来表达强烈的感情。有一张很流行的动图主角是演员、歌手克里斯蒂娜·阿奎莱拉，她翻着白眼，一脸嫌弃地说"拜托你消停下吧"。同样很受欢迎的另一张动图展示的是歌手泰勒·斯威夫特欢快扭动的样子，图像剪辑自她的热门单曲《摆脱》。

在大洋彼岸的日本，动图则到位地表现了讨人喜欢又可爱的"Moe"，"Moe"类似于"可爱"文化，也就是中文中的萌。猫叔——一只脸蛋圆嘟嘟的萌猫，四叶妹妹——动漫《生活片段》中的人物，都是动图中永恒的萌主。这种萌萌哒形象在日本被视为"天真烂漫"的象征。

中国也有自己独特的动图。兔斯基是中国漫画家王卯卯创作的一套动画表情，它也是许多中国动态图的灵感来源。兔斯基自嘲的态度深受亚洲、北美和拉美的社交媒体用户喜爱。香港传媒公司 Outblaze 创始人萧逸指出：动态图传递了语言表达不出的信息。它们一言不发却能让人产生共鸣。②"兔斯基的流行告诉我们不同国家的年轻人是有共同价值观的，文化边界正在变得模糊，"萧逸这样告诉《金融时报》。

【译文】

GIF, the Third Language

Why bother commenting with a bland exclamation? Or posting the same old emoticons on social media? Liven up your social media game with GIFs, which is short for "graphics interchange format".

GIFs are a pop culture phenomenon. Basically, they are just moving images, looped to play over and over again, for maximum effect. *The New York Times* even heralded GIFs as a "third language" for messaging. Now, every 24 hours, more than 5 million GIFs are sent through Facebook's messaging app.

① Thanks to improvements in mobile technology and a surge of messaging applications, GIFs "have become a mainstream form of digital expression, a way to relay complex feelings and thoughts in ways beyond words and even photographs", said *The New York Times*. "Young people are driving the GIF because it enhances their online persona," Topher Chris, US social network Tumblr's editorial director, told PBS.

GIFs serve as a window into US celebrity culture. Popular music and movie stars are appropriated as avatars to convey intense feelings. One popular GIF includes singer-actress Christina Aguilera rolling her eyes and mouthing the words, "Please stop." Another clip shows singer Taylor Swift wiggling joyously, from her hit single *Shake It Off*.

Across the Pacific, in Japan, GIFs help illustrate the cutesy, infantilized world of "moe", similar to "kawaii" (cute) culture, or later "meng" in Chinese. Shironeko, the lovably round-faced cat, and Yotsuba, a character from the anime *Slice of Life*, are among the "meng" characters immortalized as GIFs. These characters are perceived as symbols of youthful naivety in Japan.

China also has its own unique brand of GIF. Tuziki, an animation by the Chinese cartoonist Wang Maomao, is one of the many sources of inspiration for Chinese GIFs. Tuziki's self-deprecating attitudes have proved appealing to Asian, North American and Latin American users on social media.

Yat Siu, founder of the Hong Kong-based media company Outblaze points out that GIFs can do what language cannot. They can appeal to our common humanity, without speaking a single word. ②"Tuziki shows us that... young people of different nationalities share certain values, a cultural boundaries are blurred," he told *the Financial Times*.

【译文分析】

①由于移动通信技术的进步和大量通信程序的开发,动图"已经成为一种主流的数字化表达,它通过非文字甚至非图片的方式传递着人类复杂的情绪和想法",《纽约时报》评论道。

译文:Thanks to improvements in mobile technology and a surge of messaging applications, GIFs "have become a mainstream form of digital expression, a way to relay complex feelings and thoughts in ways beyond words and even photographs", said *The New York Times*.

"thanks to"表达的是"归因为",在听译过程中容易出错,被译为"感谢"。因为口译会受到时间影响,对原文的变动顺序影响有限,没有办法将"《纽约时报》评论道"提前译,只能在最后添加。

②"兔斯基的流行告诉我们不同国家的年轻人是有共同价值观的,文化边界正在变得模糊,"萧逸告诉《金融时报》。

译文:"Tuziki shows us that... young people of different nationalities share certain values, a cultural boundaries are blurred," he told the *Financial Times*.

本句译文中将"模糊"译为"blurred"而不是"vague"或者"unclear",因为该词具有更加广泛的含义,既有实物也有记忆和边缘的感情色彩。另外,译者对于常规的报刊要掌握对应的英文翻译,此处就是"*Financial Times*"对应了"《金融时报》"。

2. 英译中

【原文】

"Because somebody grows up being a social media native, it doesn't make them an expert in using social media at work. Companies hire millennials because they think they're good at social media. Then their bosses discover they don't have those skills and get frustrated" says William Ward, professor of social media at Syracuse University's S.I. Newhouse School of Public Communications.

According to Ward, who has 13,500 Twitter followers and teaches a series of popular undergraduate and graduate courses on social media at the university, while millennials are very good at connecting with people they already know, they often fail to understand the professional opportunities and pitfalls posed by networks.

For students and recent grads entering the workforce, some social media 101 is definitely in order. In particular, career-minded millennials desperately need to brush up on these five social media skills.

Knowing when to hit the bleep button

Last September, Business Insider attracted attention for firing its chief technology officer, Pax Dickinson, because of comments he made on his personal Twitter account. While Dickinson's Tweets on women and minorities were especially offensive, the situation hints at a larger issue. Millennials sometimes fail to appreciate that personal profiles can have professional repercussions. Twitter, Facebook, and other networks are largely public platforms; comments made can—and often do—get back to bosses. As the Dickinson case shows, few employers are eager to associate themselves with off-color or offensive content, even when it may be intended as a joke.

Using social media to actually save time

According to a 2013 Salary.com survey, the most frequently visited personal website at work is—you guessed it—Facebook. As networks proliferate—and millennial employees not only check Facebook but also post on Twitter and browse Instagram and more—social media has the potential to be a devastating time-suck. Yet it can also be a time saver in the office. A recent McKinsey report notes that social media has the potential to save companies $1.3 trillion, largely owing to improvements in intra-office collaboration. Internal social networks like Yammer enable employees to form virtual work groups and communicate on message boards. Instead of endless back-and-forths on email, co-workers can post and reply in continually updated streams. ①None of this is revolutionary, but millennials are often still in the dark on ways where Facebook-like innovations are being taken behind the firewall.

Understanding how to crunch the numbers

While millennials often have an intuitive understanding of what resonates on social channels (hard to go wrong with cat GIFs), quantifying what works and what doesn't is another matter. Should the success of a Twitter campaign be measured on the basis of re-tweets, mentions, replies, referral traffic, or sales leads? What are the best times of day to post on Facebook, and what is the optimum post frequency? Which analytical tools are best for crunching the numbers? While social media is about authentic human interaction, it's also an arena where data can easily be collected and applied to improve results. Knowing what data to look for, where to find it, and what to do with it separates real experts from mere social natives.

Mastering the multi-network shuffle

It's one thing to be a Twitter guru or have a huge LinkedIn following. The real talent lies in orchestrating different platforms to work together and in understanding the niche each fills. Visual networks like Instagram and YouTube, for instance, are increasingly the foundation of campaigns by social-savvy brands like Nike (NKE), Red Bull, and Mercedes. Catchy images and videos are, in turn, seeded onto traditional text-based networks like Twitter and Facebook. From there, links lead viewers back to blogs and company pages, sending customers spiraling deeper into the sales funnel. Meanwhile, uniform hashtags across platforms help unify and track the overall campaign. Even millennials with deep social credentials often fail to understand the profound multiplying effects of integrating different networks.

Networking professionally on social media

By the time millennials graduate from college, many have dutifully filled their LinkedIn profiles with part-time positions, internships, extra-curriculars and academic accomplishments. But the network's true job-finding power is often overlooked: Hiring managers and CEOs who would normally be out of reach are often just a connection or two away. In fact, you don't need to be connected at all. A paid feature called InMail, for instance, enables users to send emails directly to any one of

LinkedIn's 277 million members. Truly enterprising job seekers can hunt down big fish like Richard Branson, Bill Gates, and Deepak Chopra, then send a pitch straight to their inbox. ② Notoriously footloose millennials—forever in search of the next job opportunity—might well take this tip to heart when searching for greener professional pastures.

【译文】

美国雪域大学 S. I. 钮豪斯公共传播学院教授威廉·沃德说:"一个人生于社交媒体年代,并不意味着他就是运用社交媒体工作的专家。很多企业招聘千禧一代是因为觉得他们肯定擅长社交媒体。①结果他们的老板沮丧地发现,这些人并没有掌握这些技能。"

沃德在雪域大学主讲一系列受到学生普遍欢迎的本科和研究生课程,他在推特上有13 500名粉丝。他认为,千禧一代虽然擅于在社交网络上联络自己已经认识的人,但他们往往很难识别出社交网站上的职业机会和陷阱。

对于学生和初入职场的毕业生来说,学习一些社交媒体须知完全有必要。事业心强的80后、90后们尤其要重温一下以下五个社交媒体技能。

知道什么时候按下删除键

去年九月,商业新闻网站 Business Insider 的技术总监帕克斯·迪克金森因为自己发表在私人推特账户上的言论而被东家开除,引起了广泛的关注。迪克金森在推特上发表的关于女性和少数族裔的言论的确非常无礼,但是这个案例也暗示了一个更大的问题。80后、90后们有时意识不到个人言论有时也会造成职业上的影响。推特、脸书等社交网络都是大型公众平台,你在上面发表的言论经常会反馈到老板的耳朵里。迪克金森的事例表明,很少有哪个公司愿意把自己和种族歧视或其他歧视性的内容联系在一块儿,哪怕你的本意只是讲个笑话。

用社交媒体节省时间

据科技类求职网站 Salary.com 去年的一项调查显示,人们在工作时间最经常上的私人网站是脸书。随着社交网站的繁荣,现在大家上班时不仅要上脸书,还会刷推特和照片墙,社交媒体很有潜力成为职场的时间杀手。但同时社交媒体也可以节省工作时间。麦肯锡公司最近的一份报告指出,社交媒体的内部协作能力有可能为企业界节省高达1.3万亿美元的资金。比如像 Yammer 这样的内部社交网络可以让员工组成虚拟的工作组,在信息板上进行沟通。员工们在协作时不再需要无穷无尽的邮件往来,而是可以持续在信息流上发布或回复消息。虽然这些都不是什么革命性的新技术,但是80后、90后们在如何在企业内部使用脸书这类社交网络这个问题上,眼前仍然是一团黑。

明白怎样分析数据

80后、90后们对什么东西在社交渠道上能火有一种天生的理解(看看那些小猫动画的走红就知道了),但是要想把哪些东西能火、哪些东西不能火量化出来就是另一回事了。微博营销活动的成功应该拿什么来衡量？转发、引用、回复、引荐流量还是客户人数？在脸书上发贴的最好时机是几点？隔多长时间发一次贴最合适？研究这些数据最好的分析工具是什么？虽然社交媒体本质上在于人的沟通，但它同时也是一个收集数据、利用数据改善业绩的平台。知不知道应该寻找哪种数据、在哪寻找数据、如何分析数据，就决定了你究竟是专家还是普通的社交媒体爱好者。

整合多个社交媒体平台

有的人是推特大师，或者在领英上有大量粉丝。但是真正的人才是那些擅于整合运用不同平台，同时明白每一种平台主要针对哪一块市场的人。比如照片墙和油管这种以视觉为主的网络越来越受耐克、红牛、梅塞德斯奔驰等品牌的青睐。比较简单的图像和视频则主打那些传统的文字型社交网络（比如脸书和推特）。消费者们通过这些社交网站的链接进入公司的博客或主页，然后进一步陷入更深的销售漏斗。同时横跨各平台的统一的主题标签有助于统一和追踪总体的营销活动。即便是在社交媒体上造诣颇深的80后、90后们，往往也不明白整合不同社交媒体平台所能带来的倍增效用。

以职业姿态在社交媒体上拓展人脉

等到80后、90后们迈出校门的时候，很多人都在领英的个人资料栏里如实填写了自己的兼职经历、实习经历、课外活动和学业成绩等。但是领英在找工作上最强大的能力却经常被人忽视了：有些招聘经理或者执行经理虽然一般没办法直接联系上，但中间只要经过一层或两层中间人就能"攀"上关系。比如这个网站有一项叫做InMail的付费服务，让用户可以向全网2.77亿名用户中的任何一个人直接发送邮件。真正有进取心的求职者可以直接拿下理查德·布兰森、比尔·盖茨或者狄巴克·乔布拉这样的"大鱼"，直接向他们的邮箱投递简历。②80后、90后们都有一颗"驿动的心"——总是在找下一个工作机会。所以如果你想"广阔天地大有作为"的时候，不妨把这一招记在心里。

【译文分析】

①None of this is revolutionary, but millennials are often still in the dark on ways where Facebook-like innovations are being taken behind the firewall.

译文：虽然这些都不是什么革命性的新技术，但是80后、90后们在如何在企业内部使用脸书这类社交网络这个问题上，眼前仍然是一团黑。

"millennials"本义为"千禧一代"，转换译为"80后、90后"更加符合语气上的表述，也依然符合"千禧一代"所指的年代。"behind the firewall"原意是指"防火墙之后"，为计算机术语类，不译出是为了节省当场反应的时间，以免误译，并且也不影响内容的理解。

② Notoriously footloose millennials—forever in search of the next job opportunity—might well take this tip to heart when searching for greener professional pastures.

译文：80后、90后们都有一颗"驿动的心"——总是在找下一个工作机会。所以如果你想"广阔天地大有作为"的时候,不妨把这一招记在心里。

"notoriously"本义为"臭名昭著地",但是此处没有译出是为了避免语气的不恰当。译文中巧妙地将"footloose"译为"有一颗驿动的心"非常符合 80 后、90 后一代的心情。"take this tip to heart"译为"把这招记在心里"比较接地气。"greener professional pasture"并不是"更绿的职业草地",而是含有比喻用意,指"职场的宽广"。

Ⅴ. 技能训练之非语言交流技巧

人与人之间的沟通应该主要包含两种,即,语言(verbal communication)和非语言(non-verbal communication),其中的非语言则又包含多种,比如肢体语言(body language)、符号语言(sign language)和物体语言(object language)。每一种方式都会释放不同的信息给听众。比如,在肢体语言当中,大家通常用的"剪刀手"往往会出现在照片图像中,配上当事人的笑脸,表达了一种喜悦和胜利;或者当事人漫无目的地转悠显示了其所处的心态。在符号语言中,著名作家丹布朗 Dan Brown 的系列作品《达芬奇密码》中多种的宗教符号令观众了解到圣经中的秘密;或者在原始森林里部落族群使用的密码印记。在物体语言中,整齐的物体摆放或者杂乱的房间都显示出相关人的性格品德等。

在口译过程中,好的译者要能识别说话人的非语言信息,才能更加准确地对译文进行理解并且传达,所以译员要学会察言观色,而不是埋头于笔记当中放弃和说话人及听众的非语言交流机会。作为译员,很多场合之下是信息的绝对传播者,听众在无法理解讲话人的情况之下基本就依赖于译员的语言和非语言交际输入。好的译员能控制自己的声音缓急、高低和大小,在情感因素上照顾到现场需求,但是又不会过于做作占领讲话权,一切有"度"的衡量。在语速上,译员要基本保持发言人的语速,不能抢词也不能故意延后,在停顿上保持恰当节奏,注意发言人的口头禅,而避免自己的口头禅。

在各种口译培训材料中都有强调的一个译员要素就是其应该具有演讲家的风范,而众所周知的就是演讲家特别在意的是其肢体语言传达的非语言信息,在最大程度上传达出发言者的含义、情感和神态等。但是译员和演讲者有一点明显不同的区别在于,译员要避免模仿发言人的体态语言,要始终记住译员是对语言的二次传达者,不是木偶,使用的工具是声音,不必要对发言人的手势等做出模仿。

非语言交流技能的培养是语言能力之外的要求,掌握好了能更加突显口译的效果,和语言能力一样,其养成不是一朝一夕的功夫,需要更多的观察和口译现场的不断历练。

Ⅵ. 词汇拓展

关注 follow

取消关注 unfollow

跟随者 follower

分享 share

回复 reply

转发 repost

评论 comment

赞/点赞 like

加好友 friend

删除/解除好友 unfriend

私信 private message/direct message

朋友圈 moments（official name）

@（音 at）

#（音 hashtag）

简介/个人资料 profile

参考文献

［1］张柏然. 面向 21 世纪的译学研究［M］. 北京：商务印书馆，2002.

［2］http：//www.i21st.cn/.

［3］http：//www.putclub.com/.

［4］http：//www.chinadaily.com.cn/.

［5］http：//www.putclub.com/html/ability/Society/20140409/84834.html.

［6］http：//www.putclub.com/html/ability/readingProse/20150902/105936.html.